ON FREEDOM

ON FREEDOM

A Philosophical Dialogue

Nicholas J. Pappas

Algora Publishing
New York

Library of Congress Cataloging-in-Publication Data —

Pappas, Nicholas J.
On freedom : a philosophical dialogue / Nicholas J. Pappas.
    pages cm
    ISBN 978-1-62894-057-2 (soft cover : alk. paper) —ISBN 978-1-62894-058-9 (hard
cover : alk. paper) —ISBN 978-1-62894-059-6 (ebook) 1. Liberty. I. Title.
    B105.L45P36 2014
    123'.5—dc23
                        2013049446

Front cover image © Colin Anderson/Blend Images/Corbis

Printed in the United States

TABLE OF CONTENTS

Introduction

What qualifies me to write a book about freedom? What, for that matter, would qualify anyone to write a book about freedom?

Knowing freedom, really knowing it — and living it.

But do I know freedom? And if I don't, how can I possibly live it? Further, what if I know it but fail to live it?

As these questions suggest, the writing of this book was a sort of test, a test of myself and what I know and live. I had to write the book to know whether I was worthy of writing it.

So what if I found myself unworthy? What a scandal! To publish a book I know I'm not qualified to write!

Well, what's the reader to think? Surely I found myself worthy or I wouldn't have gone ahead and offered the book to the world.

I am worthy. But I'm not worthy of the above standard of knowing and living in the perfectly pure and simple sense.

I discovered another standard along the way.

An image here will help. Let's suppose freedom to be a precious gem stone. We, of course, enhance the beauty of a gem by cutting facets into it.

I started the book with the raw stone called freedom. In each chapter I attempted a cut. Whether the cut was successful or not, you can judge. But, in either case, note how the cut was made.

You see, the standard I adopted was that of offering something of use. Look to my failure or success before making cuts of your own. Let me be the test case. And let whatever little light may shine from my work give you hope that you can do better.

Nick Pappas

1 PHILOSOPHY

Director: Do you think freedom and philosophy go hand-in-hand?

Friend: Of course.

Director: Why do you think that is?

Friend: Because you can't philosophize unless you're free.

Director: But why?

Friend: Because you're not at liberty to question if you're not free.

Director: But even when you're free in a larger sense, you're often not at liberty to question. Wouldn't you agree?

Friend: I agree.

Director: So what do you think it takes to be at liberty to question?

Friend: I think it takes knowledge.

Director: Knowledge? Really? Please say more.

Friend: Well, you need to know three things. You must know what to ask, of whom, and when.

Director: You mean philosophy doesn't just go around asking the same things of everybody all the time?

Friend: Of course not. Philosophy, true philosophy, knows to ask the right question of the right person at the right time.

Director: And these three 'rights' add up to liberty?

Friend: Yes. They add up to the freedom to philosophize.

Director: Can you tell me more about the three rights? What's so important about the right question?

Friend: There are infinite potential questions in the world. But there are only a few truly important questions. To focus on anything but the important questions is a great waste of time.

Director: Would you say that questions regarding freedom are important?

Friend: Of course I would.

Director: Now what about the second right, the right person? Why not just ask everyone about freedom?

Friend: Not everyone sees freedom as admitting of question.

Director: You mean they take it for granted?

Friend: Yes. People don't question what they take for granted.

Director: Then what about the third right, the right time?

Friend: The right time is when the thing in question is in danger.

Director: In danger? Is freedom in danger now?

Friend: I think it is. Don't you?

Director: I'm not sure, Friend. Sometimes freedom seems to me to be thriving. But then sometimes freedom seems to me to be dying. Perhaps that makes me just the right person to talk about freedom with. And perhaps now is just the right time since we're both aware that freedom might be in danger.

Friend: I think we have the three rights right here and now.

Director: Good. But let's go back to the second right for a moment, the right person. If it's true that freedom is in danger, shouldn't we alert those who take freedom for granted? I mean, don't they need to know? Wouldn't knowing mean they wouldn't take freedom for granted any longer? And if they don't take freedom for granted, doesn't that strengthen the cause of freedom?

Friend: Yes, Director — but they won't listen to us.

Director: They won't listen? Don't they value freedom?

Friend: Not as much as they should.

Director: But won't they care for it more if they learn that it might be in danger?

Friend: What can I say? I don't think they would care more even then.

Director: So you truly believe that these people aren't the right people — right, that is, as far as philosophy is concerned?

Friend: That's right — and for more than one reason.

Director: Oh?

Friend: It's likely they would resent our questioning concerning freedom.

Director: Resent it? Why?

Friend: Because we are, in effect, asking them to think.

Director: And they resent being asked to think?

Friend: You ask that question as if you didn't know the answer.

Director: Well, I think we're in luck.

Friend: How so?

Director: If we stand by our three rights — the right question of the right person at the right time — don't we have the ability to protect ourselves against resentment?

Friend: I think we do.

Director: And a philosophy free from resentment is a philosophy free to philosophize?

Friend: Yes.

Director: So philosophy must take pains about its rights.

Friend: Agreed.

Director: But we really should count ourselves as lucky, Friend.

Friend: Why?

Director: Because all of our philosophy is oral. Can you imagine if we were to try and set things down to rights in a book?

Friend: We'd have to take great care.

Director: Indeed. Now let's see about these questions concerning freedom.

2 SLAVERY I

Director: What is the opposite of freedom?

Friend: Slavery.

Director: And what is slavery?

Friend: It's when your life is not your own.

Director: What does this mean, your life is not your own?

Friend: Somebody else makes the important decisions for you.

Director: Oh, I thought you were going to say that someone owns you.

Friend: Well, if someone is making the important decisions for you, they do, in effect, own you, regardless of whether they own you legally or not.

Director: So it's possible for there to be slavery, in effect, even though there is no slavery by law?

Friend: Of course.

Director: Can you give me an example of such a slave?

Friend: An example? Just think of anyone who doesn't have backbone enough to stand up and make his own decisions. He is a slave.

Director: I see. And is it possible for this slave to be a slave to more than one person?

Friend: What do you mean?

Director: Couldn't someone be a slave, as they say, to society?

Friend: You mean he makes all his decisions based upon what other people will think?

Director: Yes. Is that person a slave?

Friend: Certainly he is.

Director: But in order to be free he must make his decisions based on...what?

Friend: Based on what he, and he alone, thinks.

Director: So if you can't think you can't be free?

Friend: That's right. But thinking is only the half of it.

Director: What's the other half?

Friend: Having the courage to act on what you think.

Director: Are you suggesting that there are many thinking slaves?

Friend: Don't you think there are? Thinking is easy. It's acting that's hard.

Director: I'm not so sure about that, Friend. Oh, I agree that acting can be hard. But I don't know that thinking is always easy.

Friend: Why?

Director: Look at it this way. Would you agree that speaking is a sort of acting?

Friend: Talk is cheap.

Director: Sometimes. But consider this. If you're a slave, in effect, and you have a master, in effect, would it be easy to assert your independence from him in so many words?

Friend: Of course not.

Director: And that assertion comes by means of talk?

Friend: Yes.

Director: So talk isn't easy or cheap, at least not in this situation?

Friend: True.

Director: Just as action is neither cheap nor easy?

Friend: I suppose.

Director: So talk, or speaking, in this case, is the same as acting — neither cheap nor easy?

Friend: To the extent speaking is neither cheap nor easy, I'll grant you it's the same as acting.

Director: Now, when we think, what do we do?

Friend: We just... think.

Director: And when we just think, do we have a conversation in our mind? I mean, we say that on the one hand there is this, and on the other hand there is that — and so on, until we arrive at a conclusion?

Friend: Yes, of course. That's what we do.

Director: And this is speaking to ourselves?

Friend: It is.

Director: Have you ever, in speaking to yourself, arrived at a difficult conclusion?

Friend: I have.

Director: Was it cheap and easy?

Friend: Of course it wasn't.

Director: Now we said speaking aloud, when it's not cheap or easy, is the same as acting?

Friend: True.

Director: Then what of speaking to ourselves, thinking, when it isn't cheap or easy? Can it be the same as acting?

Friend: That would seem to follow from what we've said. But now I'm not so sure about what we've said.

Director: What bothers you, Friend?

Friend: We said that in order to be free you have to think, then act on what you think. If speaking to ourselves is both thinking and a form of acting, then it would seem possible to be free by means of thought alone.

Director: You mean you'd think, then act on what you'd thought by thinking some more?

Friend: Exactly. But you have to get out of your head at some point or you'll never be free. And yes, I concede that speaking, or writing, or any other form of expression of what you think, that isn't cheap or easy, amounts to getting out of your head.

Director: So if we're bold enough and decide to express ourselves to others, what we truly think, in whatever manner — to that extent we're free?

Friend: To that extent we're free.

3 SPEECH

Director: What is freedom of speech?

Friend: The guarantee that the government won't stop you from saying what you like.

Director: As long as it's true?

Friend: Well, yes, I suppose people can sue you if they can prove you caused them harm through lies you've told.

Director: Are you suggesting it's alright to harm as long as you're telling the truth?

Friend: We're free to tell the truth, and if that causes harm, then I suppose we're free to cause harm.

Director: But really, does speaking the truth ever truly harm? Isn't speaking the truth always good?

Friend: You know what they say. Sometimes the truth hurts.

Director: But then isn't the truth simply painful at times, like much needed surgery? It hurts, but you wouldn't say it's a harm. It makes you better.

Friend: Yes, I think that's more how it is.

Director: Is that how you exercise your freedom of speech, Friend — like a surgeon who makes people well through his skill?

Friend: I don't think about it like that, Director. I just speak.

Director: Do you speak the false?

Friend: At times.

Director: But don't you harm people when you speak the false?

Friend: No, I don't.

Director: I don't understand. Doesn't the false always harm?

Friend: Suppose I tell someone that he looks good, when in fact he doesn't. Does that harm?

Director: It's hard to say.

Friend: Hard to say? What harm could there be?

Director: You encourage a false self-image. Surely you think a false self-image can be a harm.

Friend: Would you tell the person that he doesn't look good?

Director: It would depend on the circumstances. But I think there's a good chance I would, as tactfully as possible.

Friend: Even if you hurt his feelings?

Director: Didn't we just say that hurt isn't harm?

Friend: Well, look. This isn't really what freedom of speech is all about.

Director: What's it about?

Friend: Political things.

Director: You mean whether someone in government is good or bad?

Friend: Of course.

Director: So if I go around saying someone is a bad politician, and this harms his reputation, he can't sue me to get me to stop?

Friend: No, he can't. You're just offering your opinion. You're free to speak that.

Director: Even though he's really a good politician and I keep saying he's bad?

Friend: Good and bad don't really count like that.

Director: But what could count more than good and bad?

Friend: People have different opinions about good and bad.

Director: So that means there's no truth to good and bad?

Friend: Of course there is. But I think we're missing the point.

Director: What's the point?

Friend: You're free to express your opinion, but you're not free to make up facts.

Director: Would it be making up a fact to yell "Fire!" in a crowed movie theater when there is in fact no fire?

Friend: Yes, and that's a great example of when you're not free to speak. People might panic and rush to the exits and cause harm to one another.

Director: So what's the political equivalent of yelling fire in the theater?

Friend: The political equivalent? I'm not sure there is one.

Director: So we can yell fire all we want, politically speaking, even though there's no fire? I mean, we can holler that the country is in great danger until we're blue in the face, regardless of whether or not it actually is?

Friend: We can.

Director: But let's take it a bit further. Suppose there is general agreement that the country is in fact on fire. Can we, through speech, pour gasoline on the flames?

Friend: Well, in extreme circumstances extreme measures might be needed concerning speech.

Director: So, as with the theater, freedom of speech is not an absolute?

Friend: No, it's not. The safety and the well-being of the people, on the other hand, is.

Director: And do the people have a say concerning their safety and their well-being?

Friend: Of course.

Director: So they would be the ones to decide whether a situation is extremely dangerous?

Friend. Yes, through their elected officials.

Director: Would it matter to these officials that the fuel that someone pours on the flames is in fact truth?

Friend: If the fire were bad enough? It wouldn't matter. They would silence this speaker of truth.

Director: But do we really want that?

Friend: You mean, do we value truth above putting out the flames? Let's hope we never have to make the choice.

4 RESPONSIBILITY

Friend: With freedom comes responsibility.

Director: Always?

Friend: Always.

Director: But can you mean that when we are granted freedom we automatically become responsible, act responsibly?

Friend: Of course not. We take people's freedom away because they don't act responsibly.

Director: You mean like having your license to drive suspended?

Friend: Yes, or going to jail.

Director: So the responsibility is the condition on which we are granted the freedom.

Friend: Precisely.

Director: And most people manage to keep their freedoms?

Friend. Yes.

Director: Then that means that most people manage to live up to their responsibilities?

Friend: That's right.

Director: Is it difficult for them to do this?

Friend: I don't think it is.

Director: It's easy being free?

Friend: Well, we're only talking about freedom in a narrow sense.

Director: In a broad sense it's difficult to remain free?

Friend: Very difficult.

Director: Because freedom in a broad sense involves great responsibility?

Friend: It does.

Director: Responsibility as great as making life and death decisions?

Friend: In some cases, yes.

Director: In those cases, for the people whose job it is to make life and death decisions on a routine basis, would you say their responsibilities are about as heavy as they get?

Friend: Of course.

Director: And are their freedoms correspondingly greater because of them?

Friend: I'm not sure. What freedoms would they have over and above what everyone else has?

Director: Can we say that their very ability to make life and death decisions is a freedom?

Friend: We can, but it doesn't sound right.

Director: Why not?

Friend: Because making the decision is more of a responsibility than a freedom.

Director: So what freedom might they have that goes along with their heavy burden of responsibility? Or do they really have no more freedom than the others who have less responsibility?

Friend: I guess they have no more. But there is something they have that goes with what they do.

Director: What?

Friend: They take a certain pride or satisfaction in their work, precisely because the responsibility is great.

Director: And this pride or satisfaction doesn't have anything to do with extra freedom?

Friend: No, it doesn't.

Director: So there can be no freedoms without corresponding responsibilities, but there can be responsibilities without corresponding freedoms?

Friend: Yes, I think that's true.

Director: And when people take on extra responsibilities, do they always do so for the sake of pride or satisfaction?

Friend: Many times, but not always.

Director: Why else might they take them on?

Friend: For extra money.

Director: That makes me wonder, Friend. Would you say money is a source of freedom? I mean, doesn't having money allow you to have and do certain things, important things?

Friend: Yes, that's true. But pride and satisfaction are more important than money.

Director: And yet the same freedom, the freedom to take on extra responsibilities, allows us to obtain pride and satisfaction as well as money.

Friend: Are you suggesting that money is as important as pride and satisfaction, that we should strive for all three?

Director: All things being equal, doesn't that seem best?

Friend: It does seem best. But all things aren't always equal.

Director: So if you had to choose, you'd choose pride and satisfaction over money. But not everyone uses this freedom we're talking about in the same way, you know.

Friend: You mean they'd choose money over pride and satisfaction?

Director: No, I mean that the very freedom that allows us to take on extra responsibilities also allows us to take on no extra responsibilities at all, if that's what we prefer. And here's the funny thing. I know some people who take on nothing extra who seem more or less satisfied with themselves and even a little proud. How do we account for that?

Friend: They're probably just satisfied with and proud of being who they are.

Director: You mean to say that they just live up to the responsibilities of being themselves?

Friend: Yes.

Director: But, Friend, do you think being yourself can be a serious responsibility?

Friend: I do. And for some I think it's responsibility enough.

5 NOTHING

Friend: The freedom to do nothing.

Director: That's the freedom you value most?

Friend: And what's wrong with that? Are you one of those people who always have to be doing something?

Director: Aren't we all?

Friend: Of course not. I, for one, enjoy my sweet nothing.

Director: But aren't you always doing something when you're doing what you're calling nothing? I mean, what do you do when you do nothing?

Friend: I stop to smell the roses.

Director: But smelling roses isn't nothing. It's smelling roses. What else do you do when you're doing nothing?

Friend: I vegetate in front of the television.

Director: But is vegetating, as you put it, really and truly nothing? Isn't watching television something? What else do you do?

Friend: Sometimes I just sit and think.

Director: Well, you must know that I'm the last person who would say that thinking is doing nothing. Shall we go on with more examples or is the point clear enough?

Friend: You've made it clear enough. I don't, strictly speaking, do nothing when I say I'm doing nothing.

Director: Can we go a step further? Do you think it's ever even possible to do nothing, strictly speaking? Aren't we always doing something, even if we're just sleeping?

Friend: I suppose that even if we're just breathing we're doing something, in your sense.

Director: Yes, that's true. Even mere living is something, isn't it?

Friend: Of course it is, if we're going to be literal about this.

Director: And if we are, can't we conclude that it isn't possible for someone who's alive to do nothing?

Friend: Yes, why not? It isn't possible to do nothing. We're always doing something.

Director: So what does this freedom you value so highly, this freedom to do nothing, so to speak, actually amount to?

Friend: Having time to do whatever you want.

Director: Because most of the time you can't do whatever you want?

Friend: Exactly.

Director: And that's because most of the time you are compelled to do things you don't want to do?

Friend: Yes.

Director: But when compulsion is absent it's as if a heavy weight were lifted from your shoulders?

Friend: Just so.

Director: And to go from heavy weight to no weight is to go from something to nothing?

Friend: It certainly is.

Director: It seems we're onto something here. But let's look at it just a bit differently. Tell me. Would you say that being compelled is having something done to you? Or would you say that being compelled is somehow different than having something done to you?

Friend: No, being compelled is having something done to you.

Director: What's the opposite of having something done to you?

Friend: Having nothing done to you.

Director: So while we can't do nothing, we can have nothing done to us?

Friend: Yes, that's true.

Director: Then the freedom to do nothing really means having nothing done to us? Or is that too broad a statement?

Friend: No, it's not too broad. That's precisely what it means.

Director: And who is it that does nothing to us?

Friend: Why, everyone.

Director: So we can't be free unless everyone, every single person in the whole wide world, leaves us alone?

Friend: You're being very literal again, but I think you're right.

Director: Well, let me be literal yet again and ask you this. Aren't we ourselves part of everyone? Or does everyone mean everyone but us?

Friend: Let's say it means everyone including us.

Director: Alright. So if we're to be free, we, too, must do nothing to ourselves?

Friend: I suppose that follows. But what can we do to ourselves that would make us un-free?

Director: Anything that would prevent us from doing the things you mentioned that you do when you're doing nothing.

Friend: So if I plug my nose, I can't sniff roses?

Director: Ah, I see you're going to the heart of the matter.

Friend: Yes, I am. So what's the answer?

Director: Yes, plugging your nose will make it so you can't sniff roses.

Friend: And if I cover my eyes, I can't watch television?

Director: That's right. But now comes the interesting part.

Friend: Thinking.

Director: Yes, thinking. What can you do to yourself so you can't think?

Friend: I suppose you can stifle thought.

Director: And how do you do that?

Friend: You will yourself not to think, or not to think about certain things.

Director: Now, someone else can plug your nose or cover your eyes. But can someone else force you not to think?

Friend: No. But someone can persuade you that it's best not to think. And that seems worse.

6 OPEN AND FREE

Friend: He is open and free.

Director: What does that mean?

Friend: He is as you see him — himself.

Director: But what does it mean to be yourself?

Friend: It means you don't compromise who you are.

Director: And how do you compromise who you are?

Friend: You just... compromise who you are!

Director: Is it only the open and free who don't compromise themselves?

Friend: Well, no, not necessarily.

Director: Would you say that someone who is closed can be without compromise?

Friend: I suppose.

Director: But you don't like people who are closed?

Friend: No, I have to admit that I don't.

Director: Why do you prefer the open?

Friend: Because it's a joy to be around them.

Director: Is it the same kind of joy you find when around certain sorts of children?

Friend: Yes, you've put your finger on it. There's a certain freshness, a certain connection with life that's wonderful to behold.

Director: And someone who's closed lacks this freshness?

Friend: Of course.

Director: Can we do anything to help open such a person up?

Friend: I think that's very difficult.

Director: Well, what would we have to do?

Friend: Show him that he's in a safe environment, that he can come out of his shell.

Director: And if that's not enough?

Friend: You mean he's in his shell for more than reasons of safety?

Director: Yes. What if he actually enjoys being in his shell?

Friend: Enjoys it?

Director: What can I say? It seems possible to me. What do you think?

Friend: I think we'll just have to show him that he'll enjoy being out of the shell more than being in it.

Director: How do we do that?

Friend: We show him the benefits of living up to the ideal of openness.

Director: The freshness, the connection with life?

Friend: Yes, exactly.

Director: And the bringing of joy to others?

Friend: That, too.

Director: What do we tell him if he asks us what exactly the ideal of openness is?

Friend: That's simple. We tell him openness means to let his natural reaction to things show.

Director: You mean not to have a poker face?

Friend: Yes, just that.

Director: And we'll tell him that the absence of a poker face alone will bring him the good things we showed him?

Friend: Yes.

Director: But what if he says it's sometimes useful to have a poker face?

Friend: It's only useful when you're where you don't belong.

Director: What do you mean?

Friend: It's useful when you're around people who don't appreciate you.

Director: Then we should tell him that if he wants to remain open he has to limit himself as much as possible to being around people who appreciate him?

Friend: That's exactly what we should tell him.

Director: But even when he's around people who appreciate him, won't he, out of long habit, be likely to keep on the poker face that is his shell?

Friend: Well, here's the thing. When you're hiding in your shell, people can't appreciate you. You have to take a chance and open up a bit. Then, if you're around people who appreciate the part of you that you let show, everything changes — because your poker face starts to melt away. Like a smile you simply can't suppress, the more you're appreciated the more you reveal. And if you're with the right people, eventually, the rest of you, the real you, comes through.

Director: But what if he's afraid the others who appreciate him will remain in their shells?

Friend: There's nothing to worry about. When you truly appreciate someone you can't help but come out of your shell, if only a little bit. And so, we can tell him, when he appreciates the part of them that shows, they'll smile and start to really come out of their shells as well.

Director: That sounds wonderful, Friend. So in this mutual appreciation no poker face is possible?

Friend: That's right — no poker face is possible.

Director: And if no poker face, no poker?

Friend: Right.

Director: But now I wonder what you'll think about this. What if our friend loves, absolutely loves to play poker?

Friend: Well, he has a choice. He can play or he can be open. But he can't have it both ways.

Director: But can't he? Can't we tell him to play with those who don't appreciate him, and enjoy the game to the fullest? But when he's around those who do appreciate him, can't we tell him to stop the game, open up, and enjoy his friends? Or is it all or nothing either way?

7 Expression

Friend: We all have the freedom to express ourselves.

Director: But what does that mean?

Friend: What do you mean?

Director: I mean, when we express what do we express? Ourselves?

Friend: Of course.

Director: Do we have to know ourselves in order to express ourselves?

Friend: Well, that would only make sense.

Director: Do you think it's easy to know yourself?

Friend: No, I don't think so.

Director: So it isn't easy to express yourself either?

Friend: But people express themselves every day, all the time.

Director: But what if they're really expressing something other than themselves?

Friend: What could they be expressing?

Director: Opinions.

Friend: You mean as opposed to knowledge.

Director: That's right.

Friend: And someone who knows himself has knowledge of himself, while someone who doesn't know himself has mere opinions about himself?

Director: Doesn't that seem to make sense to you?

Friend: It does. So how do you go from opinion about yourself to knowledge?

Director: Maybe you just keep on trying to express yourself, and learn as you go.

Friend: But in order to learn you would have to have as a listener someone who knows that you don't know yourself, someone who can correct you — someone who knows you.

Director: Are you saying that you believe it's possible to know someone better than he knows himself?

Friend: I am. Don't you believe it's possible?

Director: It certainly seems it's possible at times.

Friend: Then that's what you'd need — someone who knows you better than you know yourself.

Director: And once you know yourself you're free, free to express yourself?

Friend: That's right. And until you have such freedom you're a slave to your own opinions.

Director: Because even though you're talking you're not really expressing yourself, strictly speaking.

Friend: Yes, you're just opining.

Director: Now, doesn't it seem that that's what most people think freedom of expression is all about, the freedom to opine?

Friend: It does.

Director: And it's all to no real purpose unless those who opine come to know the truth?

Friend: That's true.

Director: So would you say there is a duty incumbent upon those who know the truth about those who opine, a duty to bring them to the truth about themselves?

Friend: I would.

Director: Is there a freedom that corresponds to this duty?

Friend: I think there is. It's the freedom to correct those who don't know themselves. It's the freedom to speak freely.

Director: And do those who know simply go around correcting others without knowing themselves? Or must they know themselves in addition to the others?

Friend: Of course they must know themselves.

Director: Could speaking about themselves, speaking freely and truly, be enough to help bring those who don't know themselves to know themselves?

Friend: I don't think everyone would take the hint, if you know what I mean.

Director: Well then, how do the knowers proceed?

Friend: They point out contradictions between what the others say and do.

Director: Are you suggesting that the ones who merely opine are hypocrites?

Friend: Yes.

Director: But does hypocrisy always go along with lack of knowledge of self?

Friend: Doesn't it?

Director: I'm not so sure.

Friend: Why not?

Director: Can't you be better than you think you are?

Friend: You have a point. You can.

Director: While hypocrites are worse than they think they are?

Friend: They are.

Director: How does a knower help one who doesn't know himself but isn't a hypocrite?

Friend: He's got to show this person his worth.

Director: You mean he helps him with his confidence?

Friend: He does.

Director: And when the one who doesn't know comes to know, he uses this confidence, this courage, to express what he knows?

Friend: Yes.

Director: But now I wonder, Friend. Must he always express himself once he knows? I mean, we have the freedom to express ourselves. But does that mean we must express ourselves wholly and in all circumstances?

Friend: No, we need to be able to choose when and how we'll share. It's not freedom if it's compulsory, right?

8 Judgment

Director: Have you heard it said that you shouldn't judge?

Friend: I have.

Director: What do you think that means?

Friend: I think it means you shouldn't think you're better than others.

Director: Better how?

Friend: Morally.

Director: So we're free to judge concerning things that have nothing to do with morality?

Friend: What kinds of things do you have in mind?

Director: For instance, if someone can't name various places on a map, I might judge that he doesn't know geography very well. Do you believe we should be free to make such a judgment?

Friend: Of course.

Director: And what about if we see him handling situations poorly at work, repeatedly. Might we not judge that he's not very good at his job?

Friend: Yes, certainly.

Director: And so on down the line? Aren't there many such judgments that we might make?

Friend: There are.

Director: Can we say that we have the freedom to judge in all but moral cases?

Friend: We can. But now you've got me wondering.

Director: How so?

Friend: Suppose we catch a person in many lies. We'd judge that he's a liar, right?

Director: Yes.

Friend: But lying is morally loaded. It's the same with stealing, or cheating. If we judge that someone is a cheater or a thief, aren't we condemning him morally?

Director: What does it mean to condemn someone morally? Is it enough to say he's a liar, and so on? Or do we then have to take that next step and say that he's a bad person?

Friend: I think we have to take that next step.

Director: And do you think it's in the nature of that next step to believe that while he is bad, we, by way of contrast, are good?

Friend: It is.

Director: So can we say that the real moral judgment is when you say the person is other? Judging, in the moral sense, involves essential difference. Do you agree?

Friend: I do. And I think it involves the belief you could never be like the one you judge, even under the right, or wrong, circumstances.

Director: How would someone who believes it's mere circumstance that separates the morally reprehensible from the good judge?

Friend: How would that person judge? He wouldn't. He's precisely the sort of person who refuses to pass moral judgment.

Director: But what if, for example, he finds that his babysitter has lied to him? Couldn't he judge that he has to fire the person?

Friend: Sure, but he wouldn't condemn that person morally. He'd just do what he feels is in his best interest to do.

Director: He can't condemn because he puts himself in the other's shoes? In other words, he believes that he and the babysitter are essentially the same, just separated by circumstance?

Friend: Yes.

Director: Then the real question is — are we all truly the same?

Friend: Well, some people are better than others.

Director: But don't you think that's a moral judgment?

Friend: Why can't it be a practical judgment?

Director: I suppose it can, if, for instance, it's practical to say that those who obey the law are better than those who don't.

Friend: Of course it's practical to say that.

Director: Then when we put a man to death for his crimes, it's possible we're just making a practical judgment?

Friend: That's right.

Director: But doesn't the law speak of things like moral turpitude in certain cases?

Friend: Yes, but in those cases it's the law that condemns, not individuals.

Director: But individuals make the law, and law is based on underlying moral judgments, no?

Friend: Law is based on underlying practical judgments.

Director: So you'd assert that law and morality are fundamentally different?

Friend: I guess I've never thought about it before, but yes.

Director: Well, wouldn't you say there is a lot of overlap between the two, to say the least?

Friend: I would.

Director: And what happens when law and morality are in conflict with one another?

Friend: We're in for trouble.

Director: Suppose that the law fails to condemn a criminal — a drug dealer, say. Will morality be forced to step up and judge? Is morality all we've got in that case?

Friend: No, we can still make practical judgments.

Director: Such as deciding to drive the criminal from our neighborhood?

Friend: Sure.

Director: But what if the law protects the criminal from being driven out? Can we make a practical judgment to go against the law? Or is it never practical to go against the law since the law itself is a reflection of practical judgments?

Friend: Well, there's practical and then there's practical.

Director: What does it mean to say that a judgment is practical?

Friend: I think it means that it helps us to get on with our lives.

Director: When we're free to judge the practical for ourselves, we're free to get on with life?

Friend: We are, Director. We're free.

9 Anarchy

Friend: How does freedom differ from anarchy?

Director: Well, what is anarchy?

Friend: The absence of authority.

Director: Maybe freedom requires that there be authority.

Friend: So you can't be free in a state of anarchy?

Director: How free do you think you would be without any authority whatsoever?

Friend: In one sense I think you would be free, free of any law or authority to set limits on what you can do. But in another sense I think you would be tyrannized by those who use their freedom to trample on yours.

Director: In other words, you have a sort of freedom but you can't enjoy it?

Friend: Yes, I think that's true.

Director: Then doesn't that amount to not having freedom?

Friend: I guess it does.

Director: If freedom requires authority, what kind of authority do you think it must be?

Friend: It must be just authority.

Director: And what does that mean to you?

Friend: I suppose it means the authority limits itself to operating within its own laws.

Director: Where do these laws come from?

Friend: They can come from anywhere as long as they are agreed to by the governed.

Director: Can such laws emerge from a state of anarchy?

Friend: I believe they can.

Director: That would mean that people accustomed to living in anarchy would have to agree to impose limits upon themselves?

Friend: Yes.

Director: How likely do you think that is?

Friend: Well, the tyrants wouldn't agree to these new limits. But the tyrannized would.

Director: And they would be the majority?

Friend: Almost certainly.

Director: I see. Now let's take a step back and clear up a problem we've got.

Friend: What problem?

Director: We said anarchy is the absence of authority. And yet here we are talking about tyrants in the state of anarchy. The problem? Isn't tyranny a function of authority, of the abuse of authority? If so, and if there are always tyrants, however petty, in the state of anarchy, then there are always authorities there. Pure and true anarchy seems impossible.

Friend: I agree.

Director: Well, I'm glad we cleared that up. But what about a state of pure and true freedom? What would that look like?

Friend: I'm afraid perfect freedom seems impossible, too.

Director: But what if there's to be as much freedom as possible? What would we need?

Friend: A just authority, as we said, but one of limited power.

Director: Powerful enough to deal with would be petty tyrants, but not powerful enough to become a tyrant itself?

Friend: Exactly.

Director: And is it the law that limits the authority's power?

Friend: Yes, and obeying the law makes the authority just.

Director: What else makes an authority just?

Friend: Well, the laws themselves must be just, otherwise there's no point in obeying them.

Director: So authority limited by just laws makes for just authority?

Friend: Yes, and there are no laws in a state of anarchy.

Director: So not only is there no real freedom in a state of anarchy, but there can be no real justice either?

Friend: That's right.

Director: Well, are you satisfied that we've shown how freedom differs from anarchy? Or has what we've said left you hungering for more discussion of the matter?

Friend: No, I'm satisfied.

Director: Good. But I must tell you, Friend. I'm having doubts.

Friend: What doubts?

Director: It seems fine to say that we need a just authority.

Friend: But?

Director: But must that just authority always be limited by law?

Friend: Why wouldn't it be?

Director: Didn't you say it wouldn't make sense for an authority to obey an unjust law?

Friend: I did.

Director: So what's the authority to do in such a situation?

Friend: Assuming it has exhausted all other options? Disobey the law.

Director: How would it defend its action?

Friend: By appealing to people's sense of justice.

Director: And this sense of justice transcends the law?

Friend: It would have to, otherwise how could you ever even say a law is unjust?

Director: Well, thinking along these lines is what made me doubt that just authority must in every case be limited by existing law. But the exceptions must be very rare, don't you think?

Friend: Of course. An exception can lead to a revolution. And revolutions gone bad can lead to anarchy or worse. So we'd better be careful even when we just talk about such things.

10 INDIVIDUALS

Director: What are individuals?

Friend: True individuals? People who choose to live their own way.

Director: You mean individuals are unique?

Friend: Of course.

Director: In order to make their choice they must be free to choose how they'll live?

Friend: Naturally.

Director: Can there ever be a time when we're not free to make that choice? I mean, even under the worse tyranny, are people free to choose?

Friend: I think that's a good question. And I believe people are always free, to some degree, however small.

Director: But under some social or political conditions it's easier to be an individual than under others?

Friend: Yes.

Director: When do you value something more — when it's abundant or when it's hard to come by?

Friend: Typically people value what's hard to come by more.

Director: So do you believe it's true that those who have abundant freedom to choose how they'll live tend to value that freedom less than those who have but little choice?

Friend: I think it's true. We don't always value what we've got.

Director: So, if that's true, who will likely become the greater individual — someone born into easy freedom or someone who comes into much freedom from a life of little freedom?

Friend: I have to object to your question.

Director: Oh? Why?

Friend: I don't think there is such a thing as easy freedom. It's always difficult to exercise freedom, regardless how much freedom you have.

Director: So you don't really believe, as we said, that under some conditions it's easier to be an individual than under others?

Friend: I guess I don't.

Director: It's always hard to be an individual?

Friend: Yes.

Director: Is that because it's hard to choose, or because it's hard to live by that choice?

Friend: I think it's both.

Director: Suppose you choose, and then later decide that you made the wrong choice. You go back on it. Does that make you less of an individual?

Friend: I think in some sense it makes you even more of an individual.

Director: How so?

Friend: It's hard to go back on a choice.

Director: But don't you know that some people would say it's weak to go back on a choice?

Friend: It all depends on the choice. Suppose you choose something relatively easy, but then you go back and decide to take up the harder choice. That's not weak.

Director: No, I'd say it's not. But do individuals always, eventually, make the harder choices and then stick to them?

Friend: The true individuals do.

Director: How can we tell if someone has made the harder choices in life?

Friend: What do you mean? It should be obvious.

Director: But don't you think it's possible that what's hard for one person is easy for another?

Friend: I suppose.

Director: If that's the case, then how are we to tell who the individual is?

Friend: Well, maybe it's not so much that the choice is hard as it is that the choice is one that others typically don't make.

Director: I thought you said individuals must be unique.

Friend: I did.

Director: Yet now we're saying that the choices they make are simply those that others don't typically make. In other words, the choices aren't unique — they're just atypical. So are the individuals just the atypical, or are they really unique?

Friend: I think you're being too literal. Atypical, unique — what's the difference? Individuals are simply different than the rest.

Director: Different than the majority?

Friend: Yes.

Director: So any minority consists entirely of individuals?

Friend: Of course not.

Director: Then what is an individual?

Friend: Someone who exercises his freedom.

Director: Because it's hard to exercise your freedom.

Friend: Very hard, if you're truly exercising it.

Director: So if the minority of people exercises its freedom, we can say that the minority consists of individuals?

Friend: We can say it.

Director: And if the majority exercises its freedom, individuals are in the majority?

Friend: That follows from what we've been saying.

Director: But you don't think it's true?

Friend: Of course I don't. True individuals are one in a million.

Director: A million? Then how many can you have come across in your lifetime?

Friend: All it takes is one.

11 WEALTH

Director: But does wealth give you freedom?

Friend: It can. But it can also enslave you.

Director: How does it enslave?

Friend: You know. You pay more attention to your wealth than anything else. You worry about how much you have, and how much you've yet to get, and how much you've lost.

Director: There are other things you should worry about more?

Friend: Of course. Your family. Your friends. Your health. Your happiness.

Director: But you wouldn't say you can be enslaved to those things.

Friend: Of course not.

Director: Are those things like wealth? Can they give you freedom?

Friend: Yes, I believe they can.

Director: Then why would you ever choose something that can enslave you over things that can't, given that they all can give you freedom?

Friend: Well, I certainly don't think you should. But I think some people don't appreciate the fact that wealth can enslave.

Director: They think that wealth simply frees? Or do they think something else about wealth?

Friend: No, I think they believe that wealth simply frees. In fact, I think some of them believe that wealth is freedom.

Director: Wealth as freedom itself?

Friend: What can I say? That's what some people seem to think.

Director: But maybe they're on to something, Friend. I mean, don't people know when they're free?

Friend: Of course they do.

Director: And don't they know what causes them to be free?

Friend: I suppose.

Director: So the wealthy who feel free would know if wealth is what causes them to be free, right?

Friend: But that's the thing. I don't know how many of the wealthy actually feel free.

Director: You mean they might think they're free but don't actually feel free?

Friend: I think that happens fairly often, don't you?

Director: I don't know. I'm still inclined to think that people know when and why they're free. So why would you think you're free when you're not?

Friend: Because other people tell you you're free.

Director: You mean other people tell the wealthy that they're free, and even though they're not they believe these others and think that they must be free?

Friend: Exactly.

Director: Preposterous.

Friend: But don't you think that there are some people who don't actually feel free with all of their wealth who go on focusing on it as if it were the most important thing in the world?

Director: If there are, then they are mistaken.

Friend: Mistaken about the importance of wealth?

Director: Yes. I mean, we all need a certain degree of wealth to provide for necessities and even what we might call a few necessary luxuries. But beyond that, why is wealth important?

Friend: You're asking me?

Director: Yes. Why is wealth important?

Friend: I'll tell you why wealth seems important. People think their wealth gives them worth.

Director: But don't we say that when you're wealthy you're worth a lot?

Friend: Yes, but that's just a figure of speech.

Director: True, but some figures of speech get at the truth of things rather nicely.

Friend: But can't someone who isn't worth a lot, so to speak, be worth more than someone who is?

Director: Of course. Ask anyone who loves someone who's poor.

Friend: Yes, of course. But what about freedom?

Director: Freedom?

Friend: Shouldn't we say that someone who is free is worth more than someone who is merely wealthy without being free?

Director: I think you have a point.

Friend: So what should we do?

Director: I think we should ask the wealthy if they value freedom.

Friend: And if they say they do?

Director: We ask them whether they value it more than anything.

Friend: And if they say yes?

Director: We ask them the hard question. Would they be willing to give all their wealth away for the sake of freedom?

Friend: But you know what some of them will say.

Director: That it's their wealth that gives them freedom?

Friend: Yes.

Director: Then should we introduce them to people who are free who are worth, so to speak, next to nothing?

Friend: Yes. But what if they're not convinced that these free people are truly free?

Director: Well, I suppose we can't do much about making the blind see.

Friend: But don't you think everyone can come to see the truth about freedom, somehow?

Director: At one time I did, Friend. But experience has taught me otherwise.

12 INNER/OUTER

Friend: Which would you rather have — inner freedom or outer freedom?

Director: I'd like both, please.

Friend: No, but say you can only have one. Which would it be?

Director: Well, tell me something about the two. What is outer freedom?

Friend: You know — being able to go places and do things.

Director: I see. And how about having the right to vote? Is that part of outer freedom?

Friend: Yes, of course — that, too.

Director: And what about the right to a fair trial?

Friend: Yes, all things along those lines are part of outer freedom.

Director: Including the right to freedom of speech?

Friend: Including that, too.

Director: It seems our outer freedom depends on rights. Or wouldn't you say that you have the right to be able to go places and do things? Is that somehow different?

Friend: No, I think we do have that right, though I'm not exactly sure what the legal grounding for it is.

Director: That's fine. I think I've got the general idea for what you mean by outer freedom. So inner freedom must be its opposite?

Friend: Yes, but how do you mean?

Director: I mean, does inner freedom depend on rights?

Friend: No, you can have inner freedom under any external circumstances.

Director: Any circumstances? Even in the midst of terrible war, suffering, and the like?

Friend: Any circumstances.

Director: This sounds very powerful. I'm starting to lean in the direction of picking inner freedom over outer freedom. But I need to learn more before I make up my mind. Tell me, Friend. What do you do with your inner freedom?

Friend: What do you do? You just have it.

Director: You just have it? But what is "it?" Please don't tell me that it's inner freedom. We'd be going around in circles then.

Friend: It's being free to think what you like.

Director: Are there times when you can't think what you like?

Friend: Well, some people never learn to think.

Director: Do you mean some people never learn basic logic and therefore can't think?

Friend: No, I mean some people lack courage.

Director: Thinking involves courage?

Friend: Of course it does — doubly so. You must be brave to think, and then when you arrive at your conclusions you have to be brave to hold them, to believe in them.

Director: This double use of courage is inner freedom?

Friend: Yes.

Director: But I thought you said inner freedom is thinking what you like. Can you control what conclusions you arrive at when you think?

Friend: Of course not. I was speaking loosely.

Director: I see. But now I'm wondering. What happens if you arrive at a conclusion you don't like?

Friend: You're not free unless you stick to your conclusions, whether you like them or not.

Director: So you're free if you hold to your conclusions, but you're not free if you don't? Then inner freedom involves two simple yes or no choices, right? I will think, or I won't; and I will believe in my conclusions, or I won't. A no in either case means no to inner freedom.

Friend: That's right.

Director: Well, I guess that only makes sense. I mean, how can you be free if you can't even think or believe in your own conclusions?

Friend: You can't.

Director: Then tell me, Friend. What comes next?

Friend: I don't know what you mean.

Director: You don't know what I mean? Don't we have to take the next step? Don't we have to act on our conclusions? Or should we simply keep our conclusions to ourselves and do nothing about them?

Friend: Well, then we'd be ignoring our conclusions.

Director: Ignoring is essentially un-free?

Friend: I think it is.

Director: So I was inspired when I said I'd take both inner and outer freedom. After all, acting on our conclusions involves an exercise of outer freedom, doesn't it?

Friend: You have a point. But what do you think happens if you have inner freedom but no outer freedom?

Director: You mean what happens if you're living in one of those awful times where you have no rights?

Friend: Yes.

Director: Your courage would be put to the test.

Friend: Do you believe that you would have the courage to act under such circumstances?

Director: I'd like to think I would. But it's hard to say.

Friend: I don't know if I would. I might just be content to think what I like.

Director: Would you share what you think with another?

Friend: I'd share it with you. But that wouldn't really be an act that would take courage.

Director: Ah, my friend, it might take more than you think.

13 IGNORE

Friend: You know what freedom I cherish? The freedom to ignore.

Director: What do you ignore?

Friend: The things that bother me.

Director: What sort of things bother you?

Friend: Things that aren't important yet nonetheless demand my attention.

Director: Can you give an example?

Friend: Politicians.

Director: But aren't you free to ignore them if you wish?

Friend: Not when they pass laws, I'm not.

Director: The laws they pass, are they important?

Friend: They are.

Director: But the politicians who pass them aren't?

Friend: Exactly.

Director: So if someone who's unimportant does something that's important, you can't ignore him?

Friend: Right.

Director: Can we say this person becomes important for, and only for, the moment he actually does something important?

Friend: We can.

Director: So someone or something can be unimportant at one time and important at another?

Friend: Yes, that's what we're saying.

Director: What makes someone or something important?

Friend: The important has a direct bearing on our lives.

Director: A significant direct bearing, or just any old direct bearing? I mean, the weather has a direct bearing on our lives. Is it important?

Friend: I think it many times is, when it has a significant direct bearing on us.

Director: And when it doesn't we can simply and safely ignore it if we like?

Friend: Of course.

Director: So if people are anything like the weather, we can simply and safely ignore them some of the time, assuming they have no significant direct bearing on us?

Friend: Right.

Director: And when they have a significant direct bearing on us, it's either a good bearing or a bad bearing?

Friend: What else could it be?

Director: How would you describe the difference between a good and a bad bearing?

Friend: A good bearing helps you and a bad bearing hurts you.

Director: And you can't afford to ignore a person who does either?

Friend: Who can?

Director: But you can ignore the people who simply leave you alone?

Friend: That's right.

Director: Suppose that someone hurts you but then leaves you alone. Do you ignore him?

Friend: Of course I don't. He might hurt me again.

Director: And if someone does good to you then leaves you alone? Do you ignore him?

Friend: No, I would look for opportunities to return the favor.

Director: Now what about with the law? Do certain laws hurt you while others do you good?

Friend: Yes.

Director: Would you pay attention to the law in either case?

Friend: I would.

Director: And what about laws that do you neither harm nor good? Would you pay attention to them?

Friend: You mean laws that don't apply to me? No, there'd be no need to.

Director: So you can simply and safely ignore certain laws at certain times?

Friend: Correct.

Director: But I think there's a problem.

Friend: What problem?

Director: What about the laws that have a significant but indirect bearing on you?

Friend: You're right. That is a problem. It seems that just about everything in this world can have an indirect bearing on you. And things are so complex and interrelated that it's impossible, even for an expert, to know what causes what.

Director: Where does that leave us? In the dark?

Friend: No, but this is precisely why people are tempted to do one of two things — pay attention to everything, all of the things that touch them indirectly; or ignore everything.

Director: And you're more inclined to ignore everything?

Friend: I am. But I know that I can't just stick my head in the sand.

Director: You know you must pay your attention out wisely.

Friend: I do.

Director: And how do you judge what's wise?

Friend: The only way that anyone can make that judgment — by my self-interest.

Director: But if you don't know what causes what, how do you know what's in your interest?

Friend: I can only focus on what I can know, the things that affect me directly.

Director: And for the indirect things?

Friend: I'll make my best guess as to what's important — and hope for some luck.

14 KNOWLEDGE

Friend: Do you think we're always free to know?

Director: To know what?

Friend: The things that are important to us.

Director: But what are you asking, Friend? Are you asking if there is some sort of necessity in the matter? If something is important we're automatically free to know it?

Friend: Yes.

Director: Well, where shall we begin? Shouldn't we determine what the important is?

Friend: I think we should.

Director: So what's important?

Friend: I'm embarrassed to say what I think.

Director: Why?

Friend: Because I'm afraid you'll tear it apart.

Director: Please say it, Friend. I promise I won't tear it apart.

Friend: Alright. I think the important is anything we think it is.

Director: So if I think it's important for me to know how many hairs are on my cat, it's important?

Friend: Important to you, yes.

Director: Well, we're free to count hairs if we wish. But we want to know if there's something that we think is important that we're not free to know, right?

Friend: Right. I can tell you something that seems important to me that I might not be free to know. But I'm embarrassed about this, too.

Director: Why?

Friend: Because you might say I'm foolish to think it's important.

Director: Tell me and we'll see.

Friend: I think it's important to know the salaries of everybody at my company.

Director: Why is that important to you?

Friend: Because I want to know if I'm being compensated fairly. And I guess I'm just curious in general. Do you think I'm foolish?

Director: No, Friend. I don't. But doesn't it seem we have our answer? You're not free to know everyone's salary, are you?

Friend: Well, there's free — and then there's free.

Director: You know someone who'll tell you?

Friend: Yes. Do you think that's bad?

Director: Ah, now I understand. When you asked whether we're free to know, you were really asking whether our conscience should stop us from knowing, stop us from knowing in a case like this?

Friend: I was.

Director: And you're looking for my moral sanction for an act of knowing, knowing what you're not supposed to know?

Friend: I'm sorry I didn't ask you more directly.

Director: Don't worry about it, Friend. Let's just try and figure out how you should feel about it.

Friend: Great. Where do we begin?

Director: I think we should begin with trying to find the reason why everyone isn't free to know everyone else's salary.

Friend: That's easy. Everyone's knowing would cause trouble.

Director: Jealousy and so on?

Friend: Yes.

Director: But if you knew you wouldn't cause trouble?

Friend: No, I wouldn't.

Director: Even if you discovered that you're grossly underpaid?

Friend: I wouldn't cause trouble even then.

Director: But you would go in and ask your boss for a raise?

Friend: I would.

Director: But couldn't you do that without knowing what everyone makes?

Friend: Yes. But then I'd be at a disadvantage.

Director: How so?

Friend: The boss might say he can't give me a raise because I already make too much. But what if I know I'm making less than the others? I'd know the boss is lying and being unfair.

Director: And you'd know he's being unfair because you know you're worth as much as, if not more than, the others?

Friend: Exactly.

Director: How does knowledge of his unfairness help you?

Friend: It helps me by telling me I need to look for another job.

Director: So you're basically saying you need to know what everyone else makes in order to know what to do?

Friend: Yes. And now that we're at this point, I want to run an argument by you.

Director: What argument?

Friend: When you know what to do, do you feel good about it or bad about it?

Director: I think knowing what to do generally feels good.

Friend: And if you feel good about something, shouldn't you feel good about what makes that something possible?

Director: You mean we should feel good about knowing what we need to know in order to know what to do? I suppose that makes sense.

Friend: Then I should feel good about knowing everyone's salary.

Director: The argument seems to show that's so. But there are other arguments, Friend.

Friend: Yes, but all I need is one.

15 ORIGINALITY

Director: Are we free to be original?

Friend: In theory, yes.

Director: Why only in theory?

Friend: Because people often condemn the original.

Director: What don't they like about it?

Friend: It seems to be a threat.

Director: Do they make this judgment right away?

Friend: Usually, yes.

Director: Even before they've gotten a chance to really know the original thing in question?

Friend: You seem surprised.

Director: It just seems wrong to condemn something you don't know.

Friend: But those who condemn do think they know, or know well enough.

Director: What do they think they know?

Friend: They think the original thing will cause harm.

Director: Because they've seen other original things cause harm?

Friend: Yes.

Director: But what kind of harm have they caused?

Friend: It depends on what kind of original things we're talking about.

Director: Suppose we're talking about books.

Friend: Alright. The condemners fear that originality in books will corrupt morals.

Director: But how?

Friend: By promoting free thinking.

Director: How does one go about promoting free thinking?

Friend: By questioning that which is generally accepted.

Director: The condemners want no such questioning?

Friend: To put it mildly, yes.

Director: How do they know when something is being questioned?

Friend: You mean aside from direct questions? That's easy. For instance, the hero might go against the accepted way of doing things. That causes one to question.

Director: And if that happens in chapter one, the condemner has read enough in that one chapter to know that he'll condemn the entire book?

Friend: Yes.

Director: But what if the hero comes to repent his ways in the end? Wouldn't the condemner have to read the whole book in order to know that?

Friend: It wouldn't matter to a true condemner. The fact that the questioning happened at all is enough.

Director: So if you're going to write a book that questions conventional wisdom, you'd do well to put the questioning at the end? I mean, at least that way you get condemners to read the whole book.

Friend: True, but you might get only one condemner who does so.

Director: What do you mean?

Friend: Word spreads fast. That one condemner will tell all his friends that the book should be condemned, and many of them won't bother to read it before doing so.

Director: So it doesn't much matter where you put the questioning? You might as well question throughout, if that's what you're about?

Friend: You might as well, yes.

Director: But really now, Friend. What's original about questioning? Haven't human beings been doing this since before recorded history?

Friend: You have a point. Maybe there is nothing original about questioning.

Director: Then in what does originality consist?

Friend: It consists in the generation and promotion of new ideas.

Director: Am I right to assume that new ideas will be condemned much as questioning is?

Friend: Yes, you certainly are.

Director: Why do you think that is?

Friend: For much the same reason. Condemners will think the new ideas bring harm.

Director: It sounds as though questioning and new ideas are related.

Friend: They no doubt are. Questioning, though not itself original, is the cousin of originality.

Director: And it promotes the generation of new ideas?

Friend: How else do new ideas come about?

Director: But what happens if the questioner questions the new ideas themselves?

Friend: That's a necessary part of the process. A new idea that's worth anything, an idea that's good, can stand up to the questioning.

Director: But no one questions the questioner?

Friend: I suppose other questioners might.

Director: What would they question?

Friend: The way of the questioning.

Director: Do you believe it's possible to question in a way that's original?

Friend: Now that you mention it, yes. And I think an original way of questioning might be the best way to support the generation of ideas.

Director: So if you want to have original ideas, what should you do?

Friend: Find the most original questioner you can and try to answer his questions.

Director: And if you can't answer the questions?

Friend: Who knows? Maybe you'll become an original questioner yourself.

16 PRIVACY

Director: Would you say privacy is a type of freedom?

Friend: No, I would say that privacy is something that gives you freedom.

Director: Freedom to do what?

Friend: Whatever you like.

Director: Illegal things?

Friend: No, of course not.

Director: But anything else?

Friend: Sure, anything else.

Director: Then privacy is a wonderful thing.

Friend: Yes.

Director: What if the things you want to do are expensive? Can privacy help you there?

Friend: What are you talking about? No, money can help you there.

Director: So, in this case, privacy alone is of no use?

Friend: Right.

Director: And what if you have the money but lack the privacy?

Friend: Well then, you buy the privacy.

Director: Buy the privacy?

Friend: Don't act so surprised. Yes, buy the privacy.

Director: You mean like putting up a tall fence?

Friend: Sure.

Director: Or building a great big wall?

Friend: Yes, Director, we're free to build a wall if that's what we want.

Director: But aren't there privacies we don't have to buy?

Friend: Like what?

Director: Privacy concerning how much money we have. Privacy concerning our medical records.

Friend: True, we don't have to buy these privacies.

Director: Do you think these privacies are free because they're not very important?

Friend: No, I think just the opposite.

Director: Would you say the free privacies are more important than the privacies you buy?

Friend: They can be.

Director: What makes them so important?

Friend: They're very personal.

Director: Do we always try to keep the personal private?

Friend: That's the definition of the personal — the private.

Director: I see. We said that privacy gives us freedom.

Friend: We did.

Director: Well, what sorts of freedom are there? There's the freedom to do things. We agree on that. But isn't there also another freedom related to what we were just talking about?

Friend: You mean the personal? That freedom is the freedom to be.

Director: To be? You mean to be rich or poor? To be healthy or sick?

Friend: Yes.

Director: Why would you want to be rich without anybody knowing?

Friend: You don't want people bothering you for money.

Director: And why would you want to be poor without anyone knowing?

Friend: I suppose you might be embarrassed.

Director: What about with being healthy or sick?

Friend: I suppose it's fine if people know you're healthy.

Director: You just don't want people to know you're sick?

Friend: Yes.

Director: Why?

Friend: Sickness is a weakness.

Director: Is poverty a sort of weakness?

Friend: It is.

Director: So we don't want people to know about it.

Friend: That's right.

Director: But isn't being rich, like being healthy, a sort of strength?

Friend: True.

Director: But being healthy and being rich differ in some fundamental way, don't they? I mean, we're saying it's fine for people to know about the one but not the other. I don't understand why.

Friend: Sure you do. People can take away your riches but, generally speaking, they can't take away your health.

Director: So if something good can't be taken away we feel free to let others know about it?

Friend: We do.

Director: Is thought a good thing?

Friend: Thought? Yes, certainly.

Director: Can it be taken away?

Friend: Of course not.

Director: Then we should feel free to let others know what we think?

Friend: We should, Director — we should.

17 Self-Harm

Director: Friend, do you think we're free to harm ourselves?

Friend: Well, when we harm ourselves we never just harm only ourselves. We always harm others as well.

Director: You mean those who love and care for us?

Friend: Yes.

Director: And we're not free to harm them?

Friend: No, we're not.

Director: What's the most extreme harm you can do to yourself?

Friend: You can kill yourself.

Director: And killing yourself would harm the ones who love and care for you?

Friend: It would, a great deal.

Director: What happens if you try to kill yourself and fail?

Friend: They'll generally lock you up in a psychiatric ward.

Director: They'll take away your freedom?

Friend: Yes, because you can't be trusted with it.

Director: So we're really not free to kill ourselves?

Friend: No, we're not.

Director: Are we free to harm ourselves in other ways?

Friend: You mean physically?

Director: Yes.

Friend: Well, I think the same limit on our freedom applies in other cases as well.

Director: And this goes for any sort of physical harm you can imagine?

Friend: Yes.

Director: But is that really true? If you eat things that are bad for you, excessive junk food and the like, will they lock you up in a psychiatric ward or in jail?

Friend: Of course not.

Director: We're free to do things like this?

Friend: No, we're not. The moral limit applies.

Director: The imperative not to hurt those who love and care for you?

Friend: Yes. If they see you harming yourself, in whatever way, it will hurt them.

Director: And this applies for any sort of harm at all that you might do yourself?

Friend: I'd say it does.

Director: What about believing things that harm you?

Friend: Can you give me an example?

Director: Sure. Suppose you believe you are worthless. Would that harm the ones who love and care for you?

Friend: I'm sure it would.

Director: So we're not free to think we're worthless?

Friend: Morally speaking, no we're not.

Director: But legally speaking we are?

Friend: Yes.

Director: Do you think the legal and the moral should be the same?

Friend: I wouldn't want the state interfering in our lives that much.

Director: But wouldn't the ones who love and care about the person in question be grateful for some outside support? Wouldn't it make things easier on them?

Friend: Do you know how big and powerful the state would have to be to settle every issue of moral obligation not to harm oneself?

Director: So it's best if family and friends settle these matters?

Friend: Yes, of course.

Director: Will family and friends always know what self-harm looks like?

Friend: It'll be obvious, don't you think?

Director: Perhaps. But will family and friends always know what to do about the self-harm?

Friend: You mean whether they should be very tough or gentle, for instance?

Director: Yes. And what about the many things they might say to discourage bad behavior and encourage good? How will they know what to say?

Friend: They'll listen to their hearts.

Director: And the person in question will know they are speaking from the heart?

Friend: Yes, and that's what makes family and friends more powerful than the state in these matters.

Director: But what if the person in question doesn't listen?

Friend: That's always the potential problem, right?

Director: What do we do about it?

Friend: We have an intervention with a professional counselor.

Director: Is the counselor a sort of halfway between family and friends and the state?

Friend: I guess you could say that.

Director: Why do you think counselors are effective?

Friend: They're not always effective. But when they are it's because they have experience in issues like this, and they introduce some neutrality.

Director: Neutrality? You make it sound like a battle has been going on.

Friend: These things often do turn into battles.

Director: So we have to find a way of letting all sides win?

Friend: We have to find a way of getting everyone on to the same side.

18 YOURSELF

Director: Are we free to be ourselves?

Friend: Of course we are.

Director: What does it mean when we're ourselves?

Friend: We're true to what we really are at heart.

Director: And what are we at heart?

Friend: What do you mean? We're simply... us!

Director: Do we all have the same thing at heart?

Friend: No, we certainly don't. Some hearts are rotten; some hearts are made of gold.

Director: Then, naturally, we'd like the people with hearts of gold to be themselves?

Friend: Naturally.

Director: But what about those with rotten hearts? Do we want them to be themselves?

Friend: You mean do we want them to feel free to be rotten? No, we don't.

Director: So let's be clear. We're saying those who are good at heart should be free to be themselves, while those who are bad at heart shouldn't?

Friend: Yes.

Director: How do we make those who are good at heart feel free to be good?

Friend: We encourage them.

Director: You mean with praise and other rewards?

Friend: I do.

Director: And how do we prohibit those who are bad at heart from feeling free to be bad? Do we scold and punish?

Friend: Why, yes.

Director: Who does the praising and scolding?

Friend: All of society.

Director: Everyone from parents to strangers, from teachers to the police?

Friend: That's right.

Director: If they're praising and scolding, they must know what should be praised and scolded?

Friend: Of course they must.

Director: So everybody knows when people should feel free to be themselves and when not?

Friend: Well, maybe not everybody.

Director: What gives you pause?

Friend: What about those with rotten hearts? What do they know about when someone should feel free or not?

Director: You mean, would a rotten hearted man praise someone for showing signs of a heart of gold?

Friend: Exactly. I very much doubt he would.

Director: Do you think he might even do the opposite?

Friend: In fact, I do.

Director: Why would he do this?

Friend: Because he's jealous. The man with the heart of gold is supposed to be himself, while rotten hearted man is not. He thinks it isn't fair.

Director: Is it fair?

Friend: Well, that depends on why he's got the rotten heart.

Director: But does it really matter why? Isn't what counts the fact that he does have the rotten heart?

Friend: I suppose that's true. But do you think you can have a change of heart?

Director: You mean from bad to good? Let's say it's possible. We simply start praising and rewarding the person who undergoes that change, correct?

Friend: Correct. And what about a change from good to bad?

Director: We do the opposite. But let's get back to the problem of what a rotten hearted man will praise. Do you think he'll praise others with rotten hearts?

Friend: I'm not sure how often the rotten hearted actually praise.

Director: A golden hearted man is much more likely to praise?

Friend: Yes.

Director: Does he only praise those who deserve praise, or is he at times overly generous?

Friend: I think you have a point. He's overly generous at times.

Director: Is he sometimes overly generous to the rotten hearted?

Friend: I'm afraid so.

Director: Neither the rotten hearted nor the golden hearted always praise and reward when they should?

Friend: I think that's true.

Director: And isn't the problem compounded? Wouldn't you say that both the rotten and the golden also fail at times to scold and punish when they should?

Friend: Yes, I would.

Director: Do you believe many people are rotten hearted?

Friend: A significant number of people are, at least.

Director: And what about the golden hearted?

Friend: They may be fewer, but I believe they are still significant in number.

Director: And if you add the rotten hearted and the golden hearted together?

Friend: I'd say you get a considerable portion of the population.

Director: Then we're saying a considerable portion of the population isn't always rewarding or punishing properly. I wonder what that means for our freedom to be ourselves.

19 LOVE

Director: Tell me about love, Friend.

Friend: What can I tell you?

Director: Does it make us free?

Friend: Of course it does, Director. Our spirits soar when we're in love.

Director: You're talking about romantic love?

Friend: Yes, certainly.

Director: How do you call the other sort of love?

Friend: You mean love for family and friends?

Director: Yes. What about that kind of love? Does it, too, make us free through soaring spirits?

Friend: It makes us free, yes. But it makes us free in a different sort of way.

Director: A more earthbound way?

Friend: Yes.

Director: Well, regardless of whether love is romantic or for family and friends, it's still love in some shape or form, yes?

Friend: Of course. We care about those we love, regardless of the type of love involved.

Director: Now, I want to tell you something I've heard, something you may not like.

Friend: What is it?

Director: That we can be slaves to our love.

Friend: No, that's all wrong.

Director: Why do you say that?

Friend: True love and slavery never go together.

Director: Then where does this notion of slavery to love come from?

Friend: It comes from those who mistake something else for love.

Director: What?

Friend: Infatuation, obsession.

Director: This happens with things romantic?

Friend: Yes, of course.

Director: What makes the poor soul infatuated, obsessed?

Friend: Worship of the person in question.

Director: Worship isn't love?

Friend: Of course it isn't.

Director: What makes worship differ from love?

Friend: When you worship you don't really see the other for what the other truly is.

Director: You mean you don't know the other.

Friend: Exactly.

Director: But to love, to love truly, you must truly know the other?

Friend: Yes.

Director: I'd like to ask you a somewhat difficult question, Friend.

Friend: By all means.

Director: If someone truly knows and loves you, are you free not to love this person in turn? Or are you somehow compelled to love?

Friend: We're never compelled to love. All love is freely given.

Director: And freely given love makes us free? Or are we free from the outset?

Friend: We're free and then we become even more free.

Director: But if we're not free to begin with?

Friend: Then our love can't be freely given.

Director: What does it take to be free to begin with?

Friend: You have to know yourself.

Director: And if you know yourself you know what sort of love is good for you?

Friend: Yes, you do.

Director: So are you saying that you may feel love for someone, but know that it's not a love that's good for you, and therefore you won't give your love to the person in question?

Friend: No, not quite. You see, I believe that when you know yourself you only actually feel love for those who are in fact good for you to love.

Director: So knowledge affects feelings?

Friend: Yes, certainly.

Director: And if I think I know myself and I feel love for the whole world?

Friend: Well, if you really know yourself, then that love for the whole world is good for you.

Director: How do you know if you really know yourself?

Friend: There's no harder knowledge in the world to come by.

Director: Agreed. But how do we come by this knowledge?

Friend: Through experience.

Director: Yes, but can't you experience many things without learning anything from them? Or do you believe you simply must and will learn from your experience, whether you want to or not?

Friend: No, I'm not fool enough to think that. You have to want to learn. And you learn by thinking about your experiences.

Director: What about the experience of having your spirit soar with love?

Friend: What about it?

Director: Could this soaring feeling be strong enough to alter what you know about yourself?

Friend: It all depends, Director, on what you know — or think you know.

20 FAILING

Director: You know, Friend, I heard someone say the other day that we should be free to fail. What do you think he meant?

Friend: I don't think he fully said what he meant.

Director: Oh? What was his full meaning?

Friend: That we should be free to use whatever means we see fit to achieve our ends, even if some of them seem very risky.

Director: Freedom to fail means freedom to take risks?

Friend: Yes.

Director: But it's not a risk if someone has a safety net under you?

Friend: No, it's only a real risk if you're looking at hitting the ground if you fall.

Director: Why do you think people want the freedom to fail?

Friend: They want the benefits that come with running the risks.

Director: Those benefits are greater when there's no safety net?

Friend: The safety net always comes at a cost.

Director: You mean like buying insurance?

Friend: Yes, exactly. When you take great risks the insurance is very expensive.

Director: So many go without?

Friend: They often don't have much choice.

Director: Well, they could choose not to take the great risks.

Friend: But it's in their blood.

Director: They feel compelled to take the risks?

Friend: They do.

Director: But if we act when we feel compelled can we really feel free?

Friend: More free than if we don't act on our compulsion.

Director: So freedom to fail really means being free to act on a potentially dangerous compulsion?

Friend: In so many words, yes.

Director: But does it have to be a compulsion? Can't someone calmly and coolly calculate the risks and rewards and decide to take his chances?

Friend: True, someone can do that. But I just don't think that's how it usually goes.

Director: Passion generally wins out over reason?

Friend: Nine times out of ten, it does.

Director: But aren't these people all tight rope walkers of sorts? Can they afford to be overly passionate? Shouldn't they be the epitome of calm and cool while making their way across the void?

Friend: They should, Director — yes. They have to rein their passion in when they are performing. But since you mention tight rope walkers, there's something we should note.

Director: What?

Friend: The crowd likes it better when there's no safety net.

Director: And you think our risk takers want to please the crowd?

Friend: Many of them do.

Director: So even if they can afford a safety net, some choose not to have one?

Friend: Yes, and it's not just to please the crowd. There's more of a thrill for them in operating without one, too.

Director: Thrill and rewards — that's what makes one wish for the freedom to fail?

Friend: Yes.

Director: Now I'm wondering. Do you think the love of reward can cross the line to greed? In other words, can greed also drive one to wish for the freedom to fail?

Friend: Certainly. I think it often does.

Director: And I'm wondering what else can drive one to wish for the freedom to fail. Can a certain streak of self-destructiveness?

Friend: Yes, I think you have a point.

Director: So we have compulsion, crowd pleasing, greed, self-destructiveness. Freedom to fail isn't sounding very good.

Friend: Well, don't forget you mentioned those who would take a calculated risk.

Director: Ah, yes. The one in every ten, right? So, what of them? Do you think they feel compelled?

Friend: If they do it's because they compel themselves. I mean, they're not driven by something out of their control.

Director: They will themselves?

Friend: Yes.

Director: And do they will themselves to please the crowd?

Friend: No. In fact, I think they sometimes don't even notice that there is a crowd.

Director: Because they're so focused?

Friend: That's right.

Director: And these one in ten, are they greedy?

Friend: I think they like gain. But they don't love it.

Director: Are they self-destructive?

Friend: I think they're the opposite of self-destructive.

Director: So maybe we should only grant the freedom to fail to those who are like these one in ten.

Friend: But that's the thing with freedom — you can't decide who gets it or who doesn't.

Director: You mean either everyone gets it or no one does?

Friend: Yes. That's what we mean by equality.

21 SHINING

Friend: We're not all free to shine, you know.

Director: What do you mean?

Friend: I mean that some of us have abilities that we're not free to let show.

Director: What prevents us?

Friend: Ignorance.

Director: Whose ignorance?

Friend: Whose do you think? The ignorance of those who would prevent a person from shining.

Director: Can you give me an example?

Friend: Sure. I'll give you a very basic example. There was a time when left handed people were not allowed to develop their ability to write with their left hands. They were forced to learn to use their right. Because of this they were not as good at writing as they might otherwise have been.

Director: How do we know the left handed would have been better writers if they were allowed to use their left hands? I mean, once they learned with their right, couldn't they have become perfectly good writers?

Friend: Good? Sure, Director. But you're always better when you go with nature as opposed to against it.

Director: Is it always a prejudice against nature that stops someone from shining?

Friend: Not always. Sometimes people simply fail to develop their natures.

Director: But if we're left free to develop our natures, and do develop them, we shine?

Friend: Yes.

Director: But aren't there different sorts of natures?

Friend: Of course there are.

Director: Some natures are good and some natures are bad?

Friend: True.

Director: And only the good natures should shine?

Friend: I don't think we should say that bad natures should shine. Do you?

Director: No, Friend, I don't think we should say that. But how do we know that what we take to be bad natures aren't really just natures against which we have a prejudice, a prejudice that prevents their shining?

Friend: We know because those with bad natures harm others.

Director: Do you believe their harming others could be a form of acting out against prejudice?

Friend: I can see how someone might think that. But it doesn't change the fact of their harming others.

Director: True enough. So what should we do with bad natures?

Friend: We have to teach them.

Director: Teach them to be good?

Friend: Yes, as good as they can be.

Director: And if we teach them to be as good as they can be, they'll be free to shine?

Friend: Yes.

Director: Shining at being good is much more important than shining at handwriting, no?

Friend: Of course it is.

Director: And those who come to shine in good will have learned from knowledge, not ignorance?

Friend: What do you mean?

Director: I mean, we agree that forcing a left hander to learn to be right handed is evidence of a prejudice — ignorance. But in teaching what's good, we must know what's good. Right?

Friend: Right. We can't operate from prejudice. We must operate from knowledge.

Director: And we're assuming that we can communicate this knowledge to those with bad natures.

Friend: We are.

Director: But tell me. Is a bad nature one that learns very easily?

Friend: I think it depends on what it's being taught.

Director: What if what's good is being taught?

Friend: I don't know. I mean, on the one hand, this nature should be hungering for knowledge of what's good, knowledge it lacks. But on the other hand, all the bad things it knows will resist learning what's good.

Director: How do we overcome this resistance?

Friend: In some cases I don't think we have any choice but to force the person with the bad nature to learn to be good. That's how we overcome the resistance.

Director: And if we do indeed overcome the resistance, what have we got?

Friend: We've got someone who's good, or at least not bad.

Director: And do you really believe this person, forced as he was, can shine?

Friend: If he's truly good now? Yes, but it will take an enormous effort.

Director: It certainly is hard to go against nature. But then again, we shouldn't underestimate the potential zeal of the convert. So tell me. What do you foretell in the future for the bad natured soul become good?

Friend: My biggest fear is what will happen if he compares himself to others that shine more brightly, others with the advantage of good natures. How will he feel then?

Director: You're wondering if he'll feel jealous? You're wondering if he might not come to feel that it's better to revert to being bad, to revert to what's natural? Better to rule in hell than to serve in heaven, and all that?

Friend: Yes, that's exactly what I'm wondering. What would I do in this person's shoes?

Director: Fortunately, or unfortunately, my friend, you'll never know.

Friend: Then am I truly fit to teach someone what's good if he will always be a mystery to me?

Director: Your awareness of the question suggests you are.

22 DOUBTING

Director: Are we always free to doubt?

Friend: Yes. It's just that we're not always free to express our doubts.

Director: Why not?

Friend: Because there are many tyrants in this world.

Director: What do you mean?

Friend: What is a tyrant? He's someone who demands that you believe in him. If you express doubt about the tyrant, about what he does or what he says, you upset him.

Director: And trouble follows when you upset a tyrant?

Friend: Of course.

Director: So you have to decide if expressing doubt is worth the price you might have to pay.

Friend: Precisely.

Director: But are tyrants the only ones who get upset when you express doubt about them?

Friend: No. A friend might become upset if you express doubt about something he says or does.

Director: Is the friend then a tyrant at the moment he becomes upset?

Friend: Why, no. Then anyone who becomes upset when we express doubt is a tyrant.

Director: Would you say that no one likes to be doubted?

Friend: I would. People like to be believed.

Director: So if you're someone who doubts others a lot, and expresses that doubt to them, you might not be very popular?

Friend: I don't think you would be, no.

Director: So we're as free to express our doubts about others, to those others, as we're free to become unpopular? That doesn't sound very good, does it? Is there a way not to be unpopular while expressing many doubts?

Friend: You might become popular with a certain crowd of skeptics.

Director: I've heard it said that some skeptics doubt, as a matter of principle, everything.

Friend: Yes, they doubt everything — except their principle of doubting every-thing.

Director: Can they be very popular?

Friend: Of course not. They're obnoxious.

Director: Well, I, for one, would only doubt things that I couldn't be certain about.

Friend: Certainty is for many very hard to come by. People are often ridden with doubts, even though they don't always express them.

Director: Then maybe this is the way to become popular — express doubts about people's doubts, the doubts they don't always express.

Friend: But what's the effect of doubting a doubt?

Director. You might come to see that there really is no doubt.

Friend: So if you initially doubted someone's honesty, you might come to see, come to be certain, that he lied?

Director: Yes, or maybe what you see, the certainty you reach, is that he told the truth.

Friend: So doubting a doubt just means to try and clear up your doubt.

Director: Right. And isn't it better to try to come to certainty than to live in helpless doubt?

Friend: It's better to try — but you must be very sure of your facts before you arrive at any sort of certainty.

Director: Agreed. But I'm wondering about something. Do you think it's often the case that where one sees good reason to be certain another sees good reason to doubt?

Friend: Yes, I think that happens fairly often. People bring different life experiences with them to a situation.

Director: So whether we doubt or are certain comes down to accidental experience?

Friend: Not all experience is accidental. But tell me what you think accounts for certainty or doubt if it's not experience.

Director: Before I answer, let me ask you. When you are certain about something, do you believe it's so or do you know it's so?

Friend: You know it's so.

Director: How do you know?

Friend: You know when everything adds up a certain way.

Director: When all the facts are in harmony?

Friend: Yes, exactly. All the facts are in harmony.

Director: Well, that's what I think accounts for certainty or doubt — harmony.

Friend: So all we have to do is listen to the music, so to speak?

Director: Yes, but it gets complicated, Friend.

Friend: How so?

Director: Consider what happens if a tyrant plays a tune. Wouldn't it be filled with dissonance?

Friend: Of course it would.

Director: Would everyone in the audience be quick to point out the dissonance?

Friend: Hardly. They'd be afraid.

Director: And what's worse, wouldn't some in the audience actually choose to believe that what they're hearing is in fact fine music?

Friend: I think that's true. Some of them would choose to believe that.

Director: Now, what if a brave man with a trained ear attends a performance and decides to speak up about the truth of the music when it's over? What comes of this?

Friend: He might persuade some who believe in the harmony of the tyrant's tune to doubt. And he might even encourage some who know the tune is dissonant to speak. But he will certainly provoke the tyrant's rage.

Director: So tell me. If that's what comes of speaking truth — is it worth it?

23 EQUALITY

Friend: Do you think equality is a necessary ingredient of freedom?

Director: You mean are none of us free if all of us aren't free?

Friend: Yes.

Director: Well, if I'm not free, why can't you be free?

Friend: Because I would feel bad that you aren't free.

Director: Would you risk your own freedom to help win mine?

Friend: I like to think I would.

Director: What makes you like to think this way?

Friend: It's noble to use your freedom to help win freedom for another.

Director: And freedom wants company?

Friend: Yes, freedom wants company.

Director: But surely you see the dilemma.

Friend: What dilemma?

Director: If you're not free unless I'm free, how can you use your freedom to win freedom for me? In other words, if your freedom depends on mine, and I haven't got freedom, then neither do you.

Friend: Yes, that is a dilemma.

Director: So it doesn't sound right to say that none of us are free unless all of us are free. Only some of us might be free, and we would be free nonetheless.

Friend: So equality isn't a necessary ingredient of freedom?

Director: Can you think of a way in which it might be?

Friend: Maybe if we focus on quantity and not quality.

Director: What do you mean?

Friend: It's not as simple as saying you're free or you're not. Freedom admits of degree.

Director: So some people are more free than others? That doesn't sound very equal.

Friend: No, it's not. And that's why we might have to pool our freedom and divide it up equally.

Director: Pool our freedom? So the more in the pool, the more we all have?

Friend: Exactly.

Director: But is that fair?

Friend: Why wouldn't it be?

Director: Because some people would get less than what they put in, and some people would get more. I mean, if you put in ten units of freedom, and someone else puts in one, and the pool average with all the others turns out to be three, you suffer a decrease in freedom and the other person enjoys a gain.

Friend: Maybe the freedom pool isn't a good idea.

Director: No, I don't think it is. In fact, I'd say it runs counter to the ideal of freedom, which in and of itself never calls for a decrease in someone's freedom. Or do you think it does?

Friend: No, I don't. But then how else would equality be a part of freedom?

Director: Maybe your idea of quantity will show us the way.

Friend: How?

Director: Suppose again that you have a freedom of ten, and that someone you know has a freedom of one. Couldn't you strive for equality by helping him increase his freedom?

Friend: Yes, that's true.

Director: Would it be noble to do this?

Friend: It would.

Director: And you would gain the benefit of having increased company for your freedom? We did say, after all, that freedom wants company.

Friend: We did. And it would be a benefit. But not everyone will be noble and seek company in freedom.

Director: Isn't that a problem we simply must live with?

Friend: Maybe there's a way to solve it.

Director: How?

Friend: By making it a requirement of our own freedom to help others gain in freedom.

Director: But is that in keeping with the spirit of freedom? I mean, when you're free, should you be forced to do things or should you be free to choose?

Friend: You should be free to choose — except for when it comes to helping others be free.

Director: But what about nobility, Friend? If you have no choice but to help others be free, is it noble when you do?

Friend: Well no, not on the individual level.

Director: Where else is there nobility but on the individual level?

Friend: There is nobility on a societal level. The society that makes the individual help others is noble even if the individual, because he has no choice but to help, isn't.

Director: In other words, you're saying a society that sacrifices individual nobility for the sake of freedom is noble?

Friend: Exactly.

Director: And this society would in fact be sacrificing freedom for the sake of freedom?

Friend: Yes, it sacrifices a small amount of freedom for a greater return of freedom.

Director: Then do we have to revise what we said about the ideal of freedom?

Friend: What do you mean?

Director: We said that this ideal never calls for a decrease in someone's freedom.

Friend: Well, that ideal isn't the only ideal we have to uphold.

Director: True, but in a free society isn't it the keystone to all the others? And if so, don't you think we should resist the urge to tamper with it — for fear of collapsing the arch?

24 GAMING

Friend: Freedom? The only freedom we have is whether we play the game or not.

Director: The game?

Friend: Don't act like you don't know what I'm talking about. You know, the game — insincerity.

Director: I take it you think it's bad to play the game.

Friend: Of course I do. But everything conspires to force you to play.

Director: How so?

Friend: Things don't always go well for you when you don't play. Things get hard.

Director: And it's easier when you're insincere?

Friend: Yes.

Director: Easier but not as good? Easier and bad?

Friend: Precisely.

Director: Then what's the problem? Don't you simply choose the good but hard over the bad and easy?

Friend: You do.

Director: But not everyone does?

Friend: That's right.

Director: Now, you said the only freedom we have is whether we play the game or not. But do you think this means that, no matter the circumstances, we always have a choice?

Friend: I do.

Director: And if we choose to play the game, to be insincere, we lose our freedom? We become slaves?

Friend: That is exactly what happens when we play the game.

Director: But if we refuse to play, we're free?

Friend: We are.

Director: Do you think it's possible to play the game while being sincere?

Friend: You're asking me if I think it's possible to be sincere while being insincere? Of course I don't.

Director: I had to ask. So what's this game about, essentially, aside from insincerity?

Friend: It's about treating people as objects to be manipulated.

Director: And it's easier to manipulate through insincerity than through sincerity?

Friend: Of course it is.

Director: Those who're manipulated, are they free?

Friend: If they're playing the game, they're not.

Director: And those who do the manipulating, are they free?

Friend: No, they're not. They're slaves to their manipulations. Once you start manipulating there's no stopping. But everyone in the game manipulates and is manipulated in turn.

Director: Friends manipulate friends?

Friend: Free and true friends don't.

Director: Do you think the sincere have more friendship in their lives than the insincere?

Friend: Without a doubt. Oh, the insincere might be able to claim that they have some great number of friends. But a sincere man with just a single friend has more friendship than the greatest of the insincere.

Director: But most sincere men will have more than just a single friend, no?

Friend: True.

Director: In fact, won't they have many friends?

Friend: How do you figure?

Director: Won't the sincere be friends with all of the sincere? After all, what better to base a friendship upon than mutual sincerity? Of course, not every sincere man will be best friends with every other sincere man. But won't they be friends, if only slightly?

Friend: You have a point.

Director: Now, when we're being sincere we share our thoughts, correct?

Friend: Correct.

Director: And we'd share more with good friends than with casual acquaintances?

Friend: Of course.

Director: What about those who play the game? Do we share with them?

Friend: Of course not.

Director: But are we sincere with them when we deal with them?

Friend: We are.

Director: Well, what are we sincere about? The things we don't share with them?

Friend: That's impossible. We can only be sincere about things we share.

Director: So either we share nothing and are therefore neither sincere nor insin-cere, or we're sincere and share something?

Friend: Yes, but since it's impossible to keep silent all the time, we have to decide on something to share.

Director: Do we share with them, if not in so many words, the fact that we don't like the game, and know that they're slaves to the game?

Friend: That's a recipe for trouble. They'll resent our telling them this, in so many words or not.

Director: So what do we do?

Friend: Maybe we simply keep silent about the elephant in the room but talk about everything else.

Director: We really do nothing about the elephant of insincerity?

Friend: No, we do something. But it involves letting actions speak louder than words.

25 Children

Director: Friend, are we free to raise our children as we see fit?

Friend: Within certain limits we are.

Director: What limits?

Friend: Well, you know. We can't be abusive to them or fail to provide them with a safe, healthy environment. Otherwise the state will take our kids away.

Director: And then the state will raise them as it sees fit?

Friend: That's right.

Director: Well, assuming we don't run afoul of the state and its regulations, what do you think our freedom to raise our children as we see fit amounts to?

Friend: It amounts to the teaching of values.

Director: You mean what's important in life?

Friend: Yes.

Director: What do you think is the greatest value to be taught?

Friend: Freedom.

Director: And how do we teach children to value freedom?

Friend: By teaching them about decisions and consequences.

Director: You mean we let them make decisions and then make them face the consequences of those decisions?

Friend: Exactly.

Director: But what kinds of decisions can children make?

Friend: Oh, basic stuff. We tell them that they can either do this or that, but not both. And once they've decided on one or the other we have to be firm with them. We can't let them have their cake and eat it, too.

Director: But some parents don't give their kids choices?

Friend: True.

Director: And some parents don't enforce consequences?

Friend: I know that's true.

Director: Do you think the state should come after these negligent parents? I mean, in a free country is there anything more important than a child's education toward freedom?

Friend: Well, the schools try to make up for the failings of the parents.

Director: And how successful are they?

Friend: It's very hard, if not impossible, to overcome what a child learns at home.

Director: Then why not require that parents teach their children about decisions and consequences?

Friend: But how would we enforce such a law?

Director: How do we enforce the existing laws?

Friend: People report parents when they are being abusive, and so on.

Director: Then why not have people report parents who aren't teaching their children what they need to know in order to be free?

Friend: Because that seems... totalitarian!

Director: We'd rather that poorly raised kids make poor use of their freedom as adults?

Friend: But most people train their kids just fine.

Director: And most parents aren't abusive, right? Yet we intervene when they are.

Friend: Well, there's a difference between present danger and possible future harm.

Director: Possible future harm? You mean you think those not taught how to make use of their freedom might turn out just fine?

Friend: Yes. You can learn on your own how to be free. It's very difficult, but it's possible.

Director: And do you teach yourself the way a parent teaches a child?

Friend: Life teaches you.

Director: Life is more harsh than a parent?

Friend: Typically? It's much more harsh.

Director: But life can also be sweet?

Friend: That's true.

Director: So the sweet and the harsh educate you toward freedom?

Friend: Yes, they do.

Director: During this education, how will you learn best? If all of your choices involve the harsh, or all the sweet? Or if there is a mixture of the two?

Friend: I think a mixture is best.

Director: And with this mixture, what do you learn? To choose the sweet? Or do we ever learn to choose the harsh?

Friend: We learn to choose the sweet.

Director: What if we're stuck between two harsh choices?

Friend: We choose the less harsh.

Director: And similarly, if we are between two sweet choices, we choose the more sweet?

Friend: Of course.

Director: Now, we're not getting caught up in questions about whether the sweet leads to harshness later on, or the harsh to sweetness. We're assuming that sweet is simply sweet, while harsh is simply harsh. Right?

Friend: But that's the problem. Sweet isn't always simply sweet, just as harsh isn't always simply harsh. You learn this truth from life the hard way. But parents try to prepare their children for life by teaching them that something that seems good might lead to bad consequences, and the other way round. You want your children to make informed decisions, not impulsive ones. That's real freedom.

Director: Real freedom comes from knowledge of what's truly sweet, what's truly harsh?

Friend: Yes, exactly.

Director: Then that's the freedom of parents — imparting this knowledge to their kids.

26 BIOLOGY

Friend: We're biologically determined, you know.

Director: We are? How so?

Friend: Everything about us derives from our biological makeup.

Director: But aren't we free to make choices, choices that don't depend on our biology?

Friend: It's true we can make choices. But we can only make good or bad choices. Good choices align with the needs of our body. Bad choices go against those needs.

Director: I take it you include the mind, or brain, as part of the body.

Friend: Of course. The brain is the most important part of the body.

Director: And I also take it that you don't believe there is an incorporeal soul.

Friend: No, the body is the soul.

Director: Well, you're far from being the first person to hold this view. But tell me why someone would make a bad choice, a choice that goes against the body.

Friend: It's simple. People listen to others rather than themselves.

Director: And when others speak they are speaking about the needs of their own bodies?

Friend: Yes, certainly.

Director: So it's body versus body in this world?

Friend: What else could it be?

Director: And what does this mean for freedom?

Friend: Our freedom lies in being able to choose for ourselves, for our own needs.

Director: So a free nation amounts to people all choosing what's in their own best interest?

Friend: Exactly.

Director: But what if free people choose against their own bodies? Are they still free?

Friend: I would say no. They are in mental bondage to others. You're only truly free when you choose for your own interest.

Director: And doctors, and psychiatrists, and counselors, and so on — they all help you attain what's in your own best interest when you've fallen away from it?

Friend: What other function could they have?

Director: What about philosophers? Can they help, too?

Friend: I believe they can. Philosophers can help free you from mental chains.

Director: In your view of things, how do they do that?

Friend: Philosophers deal with ideas. Where do ideas come from? People. When people formulate ideas they are serving their own interests. Those who have like interests will believe in these ideas as a matter of course and benefit from them. But sometimes people believe in ideas that don't serve their own interests. These are the people with whom philosophers engage. They show them, though not perhaps in so many words, what the truth is about these ideas. And when people come to see the truth, they're free.

Director: That's an interesting view of philosophy. But what's the biological imperative of the philosopher?

Friend: To help others.

Director: And when he helps others what happens? Certain chemicals are released in the brain that make for a sense of well-being?

Friend: More or less.

Director: What if a philosopher were to take issue with your idea of biological determinism?

Friend: He'd have to identify those who believe in my idea but don't benefit from it.

Director: Who do you think that might be?

Friend: Those who might benefit from believing in an incorporeal mind or soul, among others.

Director: Now, according to your idea, these people would have something different about their biological makeup. In other words, they would be physically different than those who believe in and benefit from your idea.

Friend: Yes.

Director: Well, if I were a philosopher set to attack your idea, what might I argue?

Friend: You might argue that there is in fact no biological difference of any real significance between the people who believe in the soul and those who believe soul is just biology.

Director: And you, in defending your idea, would seek to show that there are in fact crucial biological differences?

Friend: I would.

Director: Where do you think we would focus our attention? On the feet, the hands?

Friend: Of course not. We would focus on the brain.

Director: If you could show that the brains of those who believe in your idea are all similar, and that the brains of those who believe in incorporeal mind and soul are also similar to one another, but are different than the brains belonging to the people who believe in your idea, then you would have gone a long way in supporting your cause, wouldn't you?

Friend: I would.

Director: But you wouldn't have proved that it wasn't the very belief that formed the mind in a certain way. In other words, all of these brains may have started out as more or less similar, but it was the belief of the person that shaped the brain.

Friend: True. It seems to come down to a chicken and egg question. What came first? The biology or the belief?

Director: If we showed people who believe in your idea of biological determinism, people who don't much benefit from this idea, that you can't really prove the truth of the idea, that it's a chicken and egg question, that you have to take it on faith at a certain point — might we have helped to break some chains, to free some minds?

Friend: I suppose you could say that.

Director: So what do you think, Friend? Assuming my mind has been freed, would you keep on telling me that we're biologically determined in all we do, as if it were some simple truth about the world? Or would you admit to me that this is an assertion of yours, something you simply believe to be true?

Friend: I'd tell you, Director, that it's just a belief of mine, something I can't prove. But if ever the day comes when I can prove it, and that day may well come — you'll be the first to know.

27 DECADENCE

Director: Are we free to be decadent?

Friend: Haven't you ever seen those chocolate commercials on television? Of course we are.

Director: Do you think that holds for all types of decadence?

Friend: Anything that isn't illegal, yes.

Director: But if we're too decadent, do you think we come to harm?

Friend: Well, if you eat too much chocolate you gain a lot of weight or even get sick. I'm sure other forms of decadence come at their price, as well.

Director: Is there a decadence that comes at the price of freedom?

Friend: All forms of decadence threaten your freedom if they are taken too far.

Director: And why is that?

Friend: Because you become a slave to decadence.

Director: What does it mean to be a slave in this sense?

Friend: It means you no longer can control yourself.

Director: You're out of control on a downward slide?

Friend: Exactly, yes.

Director: And freedom never involves a downward slide?

Friend: That's right. To be free is to climb up and stand atop a great peak.

Director: What if someone wants to climb, not slide, back down?

Friend: You mean what if someone wants to eat a chocolate bar now and then? That's fine, of course — as long as he climbs back up.

Director: But a chocolate bar now and then won't take him all the way back down the mountain.

Friend: No, certainly not. That would only take him a few steps down.

Director: Do you think it's possible to climb all the way down the mountain into the valley below, and then to turn around and climb back up again?

Friend: What's in the valley below?

Director: The land of chocolate.

Friend: I suppose it's possible.

Director: But?

Friend: But you might not want to leave.

Director: You mean you might sacrifice your freedom for chocolate?

Friend: Chocolate's a metaphor here, right — even if only for a way of thinking? Yes, I think some people would sacrifice their freedom.

Director: Would they come to regret it?

Friend: You can't last for long on a steady diet of chocolate.

Director: So when they get sick of chocolate they just climb on back up, no?

Friend: If you're in the land of chocolate for too long you won't be in shape for the climb.

Director: So you make the climb in stages — many stages, if necessary.

Friend: Yes, that's the way it would have to be. But the temptation to go back down would always be there.

Director: Do we, the free, ban people from making the trek to the land of chocolate because some won't return?

Friend: No. The free are truly free, free to climb all the way down if they like.

Director: Can we send rescue parties down the mountain from time to time, to help those who want to climb back up?

Friend: We certainly can, and should.

Director: Who would be best suited for such rescue parties? Those who never succumbed to the allure of chocolate, or those who did but made it back?

Friend: Those who did but made it back, without a doubt.

Director: Why?

Friend: Because they'll be better able to relate to the people trying to gain their freedom once more.

Director: They'll be more understanding?

Friend: Yes, and they'll know how to motivate the climbers more than others.

Director: How do they motivate the climbers?

Friend: You're asking me?

Director: Of course. Don't you know?

Friend: You think that I once gave in to the allure?

Director: It's just a hunch. Sorry if I'm mistaken.

Friend: Well, I'll tell you. I know someone who lived a long while in the land of chocolate, but made the climb and won his freedom back. He tells me that it's very easy to motivate the climbers.

Director: Oh? What does it take?

Friend: Being a friend.

Director: A friend can be a very powerful motivator indeed. But what does he have to do?

Friend: He just climbs a bit and then waits for his fellow climber to catch up. Then they rest and talk a while.

Director: And then they climb some more and rest and talk again?

Friend: Yes.

Director: Why don't they talk while they are climbing?

Friend: The climbing is hard work, Director, requiring all their concentration.

Director: I see. This sounds like a nice way to proceed. How successful is this method?

Friend: In truth? Most people relapse. But the handful who don't are often among the most free.

28 METAPHORS

Friend: I like books that have metaphors that are perfectly tight.

Director: What do you mean?

Friend: I mean that the metaphors should match up exactly to what they're meant to describe.

Director: But is that ever really possible?

Friend: Why wouldn't it be?

Director: Because the only thing that ever matches up perfectly to the thing in question is that thing itself. Everything else is just an approximation.

Friend: Well, then I like the closest approximation.

Director: I think the closest approximation to some things is broad and loose.

Friend: How do you figure?

Director: Some things don't admit of perfectly tight metaphors.

Friend: For instance?

Director: Freedom. Can you think of a good, tight metaphor for that?

Friend: I can't. Can you?

Director: No, but I can think of something loose — a torch.

Friend: Freedom is a burning torch?

Director: That's the best I can do. What do you think?

Friend: It's not bad. But I'm sure someone else can come up with something better.

Director: No doubt.

Friend: Let's explore this metaphor a bit. What can put out the flame?

Director: I suppose you can douse it in water.

Friend: What's the water a metaphor for?

Director: I suspect this is going to get rather complicated rather quickly if we start down this path.

Friend: What do you mean?

Director: If we ask what the water is, why not ask who puts the flame into the water? And if we ask who puts the flame into the water, won't we have to describe this person in some detail? And then won't other metaphors spring up to the left and to the right, and even in front of and behind us? Where does the man live? How does he earn his living? Etcetera.

Friend: I think you're just stalling because you don't know what to say the water is.

Director: Well, what's the opposite of freedom?

Friend: Slavery. So you're going to tell me that the water is slavery?

Director: In this metaphor it's either slavery or else somehow produces slavery.

Friend: I'm glad you qualified it like that, because it would be ridiculous to say that water is slavery simply.

Director: But it's not ridiculous to say that freedom is a burning torch, simply?

Friend: No, it's not ridiculous at all.

Director: Why not?

Friend: Because a burning torch is a good thing matched to a good thing, freedom. Water would be a good thing matched to a bad thing, slavery.

Director: But is water a good thing when it puts out a torch?

Friend: If it's a torch that we want to extinguish, it is.

Director: But we wouldn't ever want to put out the torch of freedom, right? It must burn eternally?

Friend: Certainly. We only extinguish the flames that threaten to burn down our house.

Director: So we only extinguish the bad flames. Now let me press you a bit about water. Is water good if we drown in it?

Friend: Of course not, just as it isn't good if it puts out the flame of freedom.

Director: So water is sometimes good and sometimes bad, just as flames are sometimes good and sometimes bad?

Friend: Yes.

Director: But slavery itself is always bad and freedom itself is always good?

Friend: Right.

Director: So it seems we've failed to find adequate metaphors for these things. Or should something that's always bad have as its metaphor something that's only sometimes bad? And should something that's always good have as its metaphor something that's only sometimes good?

Friend: No, freedom should have something that's always good as its metaphor. Slavery should have something that's always bad.

Director: Can you think of any such metaphors?

Friend: Nothing comes to mind.

Director: Nothing perfectly tight?

Friend: No, nor anything perfectly loose, either.

Director: Well, since that's the case, what should we do?

Friend: What do you mean?

Director: I mean, when talking about freedom or slavery should we continue to struggle to find the right metaphors, or should we just give in and talk about the things themselves, no metaphors involved?

Friend: I think we should talk about the things themselves. In fact, I think we should always talk about the things themselves.

Director: You don't think we should use metaphors anymore, not even perfectly tight ones?

Friend: I have to tell you the truth. I've never found a perfectly tight metaphor.

Director: But your appetite for the perfect metaphor has led you to have something greater.

Friend: What?

Director: A hunger, not only for images of the imagination, but for real, direct knowledge.

29 DIRECT/INDIRECT

Friend: When you're free you can afford to be direct. When you're not free you have to be indirect.

Director: You mean when you're free you can say what you mean, and when you're not free you can't say what you mean?

Friend: Not directly, at least.

Director: But is that true? Let's suppose for the sake of argument that you're not free — at work, for instance, with a terrible boss. Can't you say exactly what you mean to the boss despite the fact that you're not free? And won't you in fact become free by virtue of speaking up?

Friend: You mean, does speaking freely make you free, if only for a moment? Yes, I suppose that's true. But there will be consequences, consequences that might make you even less free than you were before. We must be prudent.

Director: I agree that we must be prudent. But doesn't prudence at times dictate that we be direct even when we're not feeling very free?

Friend: Yes, but it's not about feeling how free we are — it's about knowing.

Director: How do we know?

Friend: Through the time tested method for determining how free we are in any situation.

Director: Which is?

Friend: Probing.

Director: Do we probe directly or indirectly?

Friend: All probing is indirect.

Director: If all probing is indirect, is all indirectness a sort of probing?

Friend: Yes, I suppose it is — or it can be, at least.

Director: What's harder, to probe or to address the main point?

Friend: Both can be hard. But with probing you're less likely to have bad consequences than if you take the chance of speaking directly.

Director: Is there anyone who is free, always free, to address the main point directly but without bad consequences?

Friend: Always? No, of course not.

Director: What about children? Aren't they free to be direct?

Friend: They generally are.

Director: What is it about them that makes them free?

Friend: A lack of understanding.

Director: Wouldn't you prefer to call it an innocence?

Friend: Innocence, yes.

Director: So what does this mean for adults?

Friend: What do you mean?

Director: If an adult who isn't free wants to become free, free to be direct in what he says, all he needs to do is be innocent?

Friend: But he'll still suffer bad consequences for being free with his tongue, regardless of how innocent he is.

Director: Why do children not suffer bad consequences when they speak freely?

Friend: Because we don't expect them to understand certain things.

Director: But they eventually come to learn what's expected of adults?

Friend: Yes, of course.

Director: This means they learn to know when they're not free?

Friend: I'm afraid it does.

Director: It means they learn to be indirect?

Friend: Yes.

Director: Is that really something we want our children to grow up to be?

Friend: If you call it being tactful instead of indirect, it sounds better.

Director: Yes, it does. But is that really the same thing? Are people only tactful when they're not free?

Friend: Of course not.

Director: But people are only indirect when they're not free to be direct?

Friend: Well, they might assume they're not free when they really are.

Director: You mean they're simply mistaken?

Friend: Yes, I think that happens. Don't you?

Director: I do. But are there other reasons why someone might not be direct?

Friend: Someone might not be direct because he's telling a lie or keeping a secret.

Director: And the lie or the secret has made him un-free?

Friend: Yes.

Director: Let's back up a step. Would you say that your being mistaken about your ability to be direct also makes you un-free?

Friend: I would.

Director: So a terrible boss, a lie or a secret, and a mistake can all make you un-free and cause you to be indirect?

Friend: Yes, all of them can.

Director: Are there any other sorts of things that lead to being indirect?

Friend: Not that I can think of right now, but I'm sure there must be some.

Director: Which of the three things we've mentioned do you have any influence over?

Friend: Well, I suppose you can tell no lies and keep no secrets, or tell and keep as few as possible. And I suppose you can learn not to make mistakes about how much freedom you actually have. As far as bosses go, that's usually just a matter of luck. But you can always try to find another job.

Director: So if you do these things, you'll be free to be direct, at least as free as you can be? Then why, I'd love to know why, my friend, doesn't everyone choose to be that free?

30 CONTRADICTION

Friend: I think we should have the freedom to contradict ourselves.

Director: You mean we should be free to change our minds?

Friend: Sure, I think we should be free to change our minds. After all, what do you do when more information comes to light, information you didn't have when you were making up your mind in the first place? But that's not what I'm talking about. I'm talking about the ability to contradict yourself, out and out. There's a freedom that comes with that.

Director: I'm sure there is. But aren't you concerned what people will think of you if you say contradictory things?

Friend: Why should I be? Most people say contradictory things all the time. They just space them out enough that others don't notice.

Director: Is that what you'll do, space them out enough?

Friend: I'll say them one right after another.

Director: While I admire your boldness I can't help but wonder about your prudence.

Friend: Why, what do you think will happen to me?

Director: People won't take you seriously.

Friend: And who says I want to be taken seriously?

Director: Doesn't everyone?

Friend: Of course not. Some people want to be fools.

Director: Is that what you want, to be a fool?

Friend: Fools can get away with saying just about anything.

Director: Then that's what you want, the ability to say just about anything?

Friend: Yes.

Director: Why is it just about anything, and not anything simply? What can't a fool say?

Friend: A fool can't say he's serious about anything. Well, he can say he is, but people won't believe him. So I guess a fool can say simply anything.

Director: And when he's saying simply anything, it's possible he knows when he's contradicting himself?

Friend: Yes, I'd say it's possible.

Director: Then maybe the fool isn't all that foolish. But is a fool the only one who can be aware of his own contradictions?

Friend: No, there are some others, as well.

Director: How would you describe these others?

Friend: They are philosophers.

Director: Philosophers? I thought philosophers were supposed to be the ones, of all others, who don't contradict themselves.

Friend: Oh no, Director. Philosophers are simply very good at hiding their contradictions. The fact that they are so good at it quite clearly suggests that they're well aware of what they're doing.

Director: And that's the difference between philosophers and fools? The one hides contradictions while the other calls attention to them?

Friend: Precisely.

Director: Then should we have fools teach philosophy in our universities? Perhaps they could call attention to the contradictions in the various philosophic texts?

Friend: That wouldn't be enough to satisfy a true fool.

Director: Oh? What would?

Friend: A true fool would write his own book, one filled with obvious contradictions.

Director: What would he hope to get out of that?

Friend: A few good laughs.

Director: But what if the fool did more than that with his book?

Friend: What more?

Director: What if he made a point to contradict all things said by conventional wisdom?

Friend: That would make for quite a work.

Director: Do you think it would be taken seriously?

Friend: Who knows? Stranger things have happened.

Director: But what if he took out the obvious contradictions?

Friend: The book would no longer be the work of a fool. It would be the work of a philosopher.

Director: And then it would be taken seriously?

Friend: Yes, most likely.

Director: You mean to say philosophers aren't always taken seriously?

Friend: No, I don't think they are. Sometimes they're thought to be fools because they go against conventional wisdom.

Director: And only philosophers and fools go against such wisdom?

Friend: For the most part.

Director: So philosophers are at times mistaken for fools. Would you mistake them?

Friend: No, I don't think I would. I respect philosophers. I don't respect fools.

Director: Then you don't want to be a fool after all?

Friend: In truth? No, I don't. But I do want the freedom to contradict myself knowingly.

Director: Then it seems you have little choice but to become a philosopher. But I have to warn you, Friend. Every time I look deeply into what appears to be a contradiction by a philosopher, do you know what I find? A consistency, an even more profoundly consistent consistency than would have been possible on the surface. So if you wish to contradict yourself, you'd better be sure to point to something beyond the superficially contradictory, to something greater — to something solid, beautiful, and whole. And if you can't do that, if it's beyond your present powers, then avoid contradiction altogether. Focus on being consistent. And once you've been consistent for a good long while, if you come to feel that there is something more that you wish to say, something beyond what others might take to be good logic or reasoning, only then should you dare to dip your toe into the waters of contradiction. And only then.

31 FORMULA

Friend: I have discovered the formula of freedom.

Director: You have? What is it?

Friend: First I need to get you to agree to a few premises.

Director: What are they?

Friend: One, desire unchecked is a bad thing.

Director: You mean like desire for someone else's possessions?

Friend: Yes, exactly.

Director: Okay, that's bad.

Friend: Two, it's virtue that checks desire.

Director: So even though I want your things my virtue won't allow me to take them when you're not looking?

Friend: Precisely.

Director: Okay, virtue is good. Are there other premises?

Friend: No, that's it.

Director: So what's the formula?

Friend: Virtue over desire equals freedom.

Director: Let me get this straight. Virtue divided by desire equals freedom: $v/d = f$?

Friend: Yes.

Director: That means if I have a virtue of one, but a desire of two, I have freedom of one half? $1/2 = 0.5$.

Friend: Right. And if you have a virtue of two but a desire of one you have freedom of two: $2/1 = 2$. In other words, the more virtue you have the greater is your freedom.

Director: And the more desire you have the less your freedom?

Friend: That's how it works.

Director: Well, that's interesting, Friend. But what if you have a strong desire for virtue?

Friend: We agreed that unchecked desire is a bad thing.

Director: But can it be bad to desire virtue? Do you really want to assert that?

Friend: No.

Director: And what about all the other good desires we have? Do you want to say they are bad?

Friend: Maybe I have to qualify the formula. It's virtue over bad desire that equals freedom: $v/d_{bad} = f$.

Director: Yes, that sounds better. But now I have a formula. Virtue times good desire equals freedom: $v*d_{good} = f$. That way the more virtue you have the more freedom you have, and the more good desires you have the more freedom you have.

Friend: But you can have all the good desires in the world. If you have no virtue they don't amount to anything, to any freedom.

Director: But, Friend, the formula takes care of that. Zero virtue times whatever amount of good desire equals zero freedom: $0*d_{good} = 0$.

Friend: Okay, that's true. But what if you have virtue but no good desires?

Director: The formula says that also means you have no freedom: $v*0 = 0$. But now I'm wondering.

Friend: About what?

Director: About whether we've got the right ingredients in our formulas of freedom.

Friend: You think we shouldn't have desire?

Director: If we take out desire, we're left with virtue alone. Do you think virtue alone amounts to freedom?

Friend: No.

Director: Why not? Isn't virtue a good thing?

Friend: It is. But virtue for the sake of virtue is barren. It can't amount to freedom by itself.

Director: Nor can desire by itself?

Friend: Good desire without virtue is nothing, as we've said. But bad desire without virtue is a monster. And monsters can't be free. They're slaves to their desires.

Director: And virtue is the only thing that can check a monster?

Friend: Maybe not. Maybe we should say that outside force checks monsters.

Director: You mean like the force of the law?

Friend: Yes, like the force of the law.

Director: Shall we enter the force of law into our equation?

Friend: No, there's no need. If you have to be checked by the force of law from doing bad things you can't ever truly be free.

Director: Is the force of law unnecessary for those who have virtue and good desires?

Friend: Well, it protects these people from those who have no virtue and have bad desires, from monsters. So, no — it is necessary.

Director: And to be clear, it also helps keep those who have more bad desires than virtue from trouble? Ones who might not be complete monsters but need some encouragement?

Friend: Yes.

Director: This means that anyone who has less than a one of freedom needs this outside force to stay in line, right? Our formula is virtue divided by bad desires equals freedom: $v/d_{bad} = f$. If virtue is one and bad desires are two, we have a freedom of one half: $1/2 = 0.5$. This person needs the law to keep him in line. The person with a two of virtue and a one of bad desires has no need for the law to keep him in line — his freedom is more than one: $2/1 = 2$.

Friend: But then what about those with good desires? Our formula is virtue times good desires equals freedom: $v*d_{good} = f$. Suppose your virtue is one half and your good desires are one, or the other way round. You'll have a freedom of less than one: $0.5*1 = 0.5$ and $1*0.5 = 0.5$. Are we saying you'll need the force of law to stay in line?

Director: But how can that be with someone who has both virtue and good desires? It seems we may need to somehow combine our equations, Friend. But let's leave that for another time. I suspect it won't prove easy to try and reduce freedom to a single formula.

32 PATIENCE

Director: Do you think patience is a virtue?

Friend: Yes, of course.

Director: And like all virtues, it has an opposite?

Friend: That would be impatience.

Director: Maybe patience is an unusual virtue.

Friend: Why do you say that?

Director: Because it sometimes seems to me that patience has a second opposite.

Friend: Which is?

Director: False patience.

Friend: What's the difference between true and false patience?

Director: That's what I'm hoping we can articulate.

Friend: Well, where do we start?

Director: Maybe it's easiest to start with impatience, to get it out of the way. What is impatience?

Friend: Impatience is when you are restless or anxious for something you want.

Director: And when you are restless or anxious, do you feel free?

Friend: Hardly.

Director: Now, turning to patience, I take it that it is marked by an absence of restlessness or anxiety concerning the thing in question.

Friend: That's exactly right.

Director: And if impatience doesn't leave you feeling free, patience does?

Friend: Yes, you're free of the restlessness and anxiety.

Director: So freedom, when it comes to patience, is a negative state — the absence of something, the restlessness and anxiety?

Friend: Yes.

Director: Then this may be a good place to start considering the difference between true and false patience.

Friend: Let's start.

Director: Will you believe me if I say we ought to begin with hope?

Friend: Why wouldn't I? When you're patient you're hopeful that the thing you want will come about.

Director: Shall we say then that true patience is grounded in hope?

Friend: Yes, and it follows that false patience is not grounded in hope.

Director: And is it the hope that goes with true patience that leaves one feeling free, free of any of the bad feelings that come with impatience?

Friend: Yes.

Director: So true patience is the absence of one sort of thing, restlessness and anxiety, and the presence of another, hope? And the latter drives away the former?

Friend: That's right.

Director: Now what of false patience?

Friend: False patience looks in some ways like true patience, but it lacks hope.

Director: How does it look like true patience?

Friend: The falsely patient are neither restless nor anxious.

Director: Why is that?

Friend: I guess when you have nothing to hope for there's nothing to get worked up about.

Director: I see. But as far as hope goes, are we saying it cuts both ways? The presence of hope in the truly patient causes them to be neither restless nor anxious, and the absence of hope in the falsely patient causes the same?

Friend: What can I say? That's how it seems to me.

Director: Then why be truly patient?

Friend: Because it's better to hope than not to hope.

Director: Why?

Friend: Why? Because hope buoys the spirit. And this allows for a certain freedom of spirit that the falsely patient lack.

Director: Would you say that this freedom, like all other freedom, must be used wisely?

Friend: Of course. And that's precisely why we say there is an art to patience, an art that only the truly patient possess.

Director: An art to living in hope? An art to the freedom of the spirit?

Friend: Exactly. Do you remember how we said that patience is a virtue?

Director: I do.

Friend: Well, all of virtue is an art.

Director: An art you perform?

Friend: You perform acts that are virtuous, so, yes — a freely performed art.

Director: In the case of what we're calling false patience you perform nothing virtuous?

Friend: Correct.

Director: But with true patience you perform... what?

Friend: An act of faith.

Director: Your hope?

Friend: Your hope.

Director: And, to be sure, hope makes your spirit free?

Friend: True and sweet hope makes your spirit free. Nothing more so.

Director: Now there's one last thing, something we've overlooked. Can the impatient hope?

Friend: They can, and do. But either they're not very good at the art of patience, or circumstances simply overwhelm them. Regardless, it's infinitely better to lose your patience than to lose your hope. So you should always prefer impatience to a patience that's false.

33 PLAY

Friend: What's the surest sign of inner freedom?

Director: Playfulness.

Friend: Playfulness? You surprise me.

Director: Why?

Friend: I thought you'd say the sign is something more serious.

Director: Play can be a serious business. After all, if you never play can you really be free?

Friend: But can't you be free but have no desire to play?

Director: Perhaps. But where do you think the desire to play comes from?

Friend: I don't know. I guess it's in human nature.

Director: Can you be truly free if you deny your nature?

Friend: No, I suppose not. But you're not talking about being playful all the time, are you?

Director: Of course not. The free are only playful on occasion.

Friend: And some have more occasion than others?

Director: Yes.

Friend: How do you know when it's an occasion for play? Is it something you know rationally or is it something you feel?

Director: Well, it's got something to do with freedom, right?

Friend: Right.

Director: And that something is that play is a sign of inner freedom, yes?

Friend: Yes.

Director: And if play is a sign of inner freedom, does that mean it depends on that inner freedom?

Friend: It does.

Director: So you'd never play when doing so might jeopardize your inner freedom?

Friend: But how do you know what jeopardizes your inner freedom?

Director: What is inner freedom?

Friend: It's your belief in yourself.

Director: If that's true, then it seems fair to say you never would play, or never should play, when doing so would jeopardize that belief.

Friend: But how could play jeopardize your belief in yourself?

Director: You might be playing with the wrong people.

Friend: You mean people who don't believe in me?

Director: Yes. But there's more they don't believe in.

Friend: What?

Director: Are you someone who has core beliefs, beside the belief in yourself?

Friend: Of course I am.

Director: The wrong people, the ones you might be playing with, lack those beliefs. What do you think happens if, while playing, these people touch you in your core?

Friend: Then more than my belief in myself is jeopardized — unless I'm very strong.

Director: Now, do you think we should condemn all play just because certain people put us at risk?

Friend: No, we shouldn't.

Director: With whom should we play, assuming the play will touch us in the core?

Friend: But why play at all when it touches us in the core? Why not just play superficially?

Director: Much play is superficial, yes. But what if there were a sort of play, a sort of play by and with the gentlest of the gentle, those you love and trust, that can strengthen your core, that can playfully affirm it, that can refresh it in all that it is? How does such play sound to you?

Friend: It sounds wonderful, if it exists.

Director: But, Friend, it does exist. There's only one thing, however, that gets in the way.

Friend: What?

Director: Do you believe it's possible to take yourself too seriously?

Friend: Of course I do.

Director: Well, when you take yourself too seriously it's impossible to engage in this gentle and refreshing play.

Friend: So you take yourself with a grain of salt.

Director: And what of the rest of your core beliefs?

Friend: You continue to take them in full earnest.

Director: You take yourself with a grain of salt because you know that you are human and therefore fallible?

Friend: Absolutely.

Director: But when it comes to your other beliefs, you know... what?

Friend: You know that when they're true they must be the principles toward which we raise our fallible selves.

Director: So it's very important to know the truth concerning these things?

Friend: Most important.

Director: Well, that's where the gentle play comes in.

Friend: I don't understand.

Director: We play by offering proofs of the truth of our beliefs.

Friend: But that's not like any sort of play I've ever heard of before.

Director: Maybe you've been playing with the wrong people.

Friend: But why is it play? Why isn't it serious?

Director: Because, my friend, sometimes the truth requires a lighter touch in order to become clear. But don't worry. Once clear there's always time enough to be serious.

34 MYSTERY

Friend: I think we should be free to be a mystery.

Director: A mystery? What do you mean?

Friend: You know, not to be fully understood or thoroughly known.

Director: Don't most people want to be known and understood?

Friend: I don't care what most people want. I want what I want.

Director: How would you go about becoming a mystery?

Friend: You never complain and you never explain.

Director: What's wrong with complaining?

Friend: It gives you away. It tells people what you really care about, how you really feel.

Director: And explaining?

Friend: That should be obvious.

Director: So let's say you achieve your goal. What then?

Friend: I'm a man of mystery.

Director: Do you think this makes you unique?

Friend: No, I know there are others of mystery — you, for instance, Director.

Director: Me? How am I a man of mystery?

Friend: I don't think anyone really understands you.

Director: But, Friend, don't you see me striving to be understood each and every day?

Friend: Sure, I see you strive.

Director: But?

Friend: But I think you're being deceitful.

Director: What are you talking about?

Friend: You want to make it look like you're striving for clarity when in fact you're muddying the waters.

Director: Muddying the waters? How do I do that?

Friend: You ask all sorts of questions that have no real bearing on the question at hand.

Director: If that's true then I see it as your duty to help me.

Friend: What do you mean?

Director: I mean, if you can see what questions have or don't have a real bearing on the question at hand, doesn't that mean you have a clear view of whatever is being discussed?

Friend: I suppose.

Director: A view much clearer than mine?

Friend: But I don't think that's true.

Director: Why, do you deny that you have a clear view?

Friend: I think your view is clearer.

Director: And if I have the clearer view, wouldn't I know better what questions have a real bearing on the topic being discussed?

Friend: Yes — but that's not to say you ask those questions.

Director: And you think I don't ask those questions, but ask others, in order to muddy the waters?

Friend: Yes.

Director: The muddied water maintains my mystery?

Friend: Of course.

Director: Then why don't you simply do the same?

Friend: I intend to.

Director: But don't you see there's a problem here?

Friend: What problem?

Director: If all you do is muddy the waters, why would anyone listen to you?

Friend: Some people like muddy waters.

Director: And those who do, don't you think they're perfectly capable of muddying the waters themselves? Or does it take some sort of special water muddying skill that only you and I and those like us possess?

Friend: No, people can muddy the waters themselves.

Director: So why do they need us? What, no answer, Friend?

Friend: I guess they don't need us.

Director: Under what condition would they need us?

Friend: If we had a skill that they don't have.

Director: I'll tell you what skill seems to be in something of a short supply. Making things clear. And do you know what?

Friend: What?

Director: If someone lacks this skill, how would someone who has it seem to him?

Friend: I don't know. How?

Director: Do you think it's possible that the person with the skill would seem... mysterious?

Friend: Yes.

Director: But what do you think this man of mystery would do with the one without the skill?

Friend: Keep him at arm's length?

Director: He would try to teach him to have the skill.

Friend: Why would he do that? Doesn't he undermine himself, his position — his mystery?

Director: The more people keeping the waters clear the clearer are the waters, Friend.

Friend: And he really likes clear water that much?

Director: He really does like clear water that much.

Friend: But then why does he always move on, once the waters are clear, to where there's more mud?

35 VIRTUE

Director: Friend, what do you think is the most important virtue of the citizen?

Friend: Friendship.

Director: Why?

Friend: Because it's in the interest of all the citizens to be friends with one another

Director: But how do we know that?

Friend: Well, I can offer a simple proof. But I'm not sure how true you'll think it is.

Director: Please offer the proof and we'll see.

Friend: Alright. What do you have if all the citizens of a nation, or as many as possible, are friends?

Director: I'm not sure. What do you have?

Friend: You have a nation that's strong. Do you agree?

Director: I agree. What comes next?

Friend: We have to ask whether a strong nation is in the interest of all the citizens.

Director: And what do we answer?

Friend: What else? The answer is yes.

Director: And so we conclude that friendship is in the interest of all the citizens?

Friend: Of course. What do you think?

Director: I'm stuck on one part of the argument.

Friend: Which part?

Director: The part that says "or as many as possible" when referring to those citizens of the nation who're friends.

Friend: But why are you stuck on that?

Director: Because it makes me wonder about those who aren't friends with the others.

Friend: What about them?

Director: Well, for one, are they many or few?

Friend: If the nation is to be strong I'd say they'd have to be few.

Director: And how will the many friends treat the few who aren't their friends?

Friend: What do you mean?

Director: I mean it's the many friends who make the nation strong, right?

Friend: Right.

Director: Who will have more say in what are the interests of the nation, those who make it strong or those who don't?

Friend: Those who make it strong.

Director: Is it conceivable that those who make it strong and those who don't will have different views on what the interests of the nation are?

Friend: Of course. But it's only right that those who make it strong should have the say.

Director: Well, that's why I'm wondering how they'll treat the few who aren't their friends.

Friend: But if those few would just learn to make friends we wouldn't have to worry about it. They should be able to see that friendship with the others is in their interest. Think of when the nation is at war. The greater the number of citizens who are friends, the stronger is the nation, and the better off everyone is. Isn't it obvious?

Director: You'd think it would be. But would you take it further? Would you say a lack of friendship not only doesn't contribute to but actually saps the nation's strength?

Friend: I would.

Director: Then tell me. What's the basis of citizen friendship, Friend, aside from self-interest?

Friend: The basis? I'd say it's agreement.

Director: Agreement on any old thing or agreement on what's important?

Friend: Agreement on what's important.

Director: So the virtue of friendship for a citizen amounts to agreeing with many others on what's important?

Friend: Yes.

Director: And those who don't agree with the others on these things can't be friends? Or can you be friends with people that you fundamentally disagree with?

Friend: No, that wouldn't be a real friendship.

Director: No, I suppose not. But then what makes for the better friendship? Being right about something important or being wrong about something important?

Friend: Those who agree on something they're right about will have the better friendship.

Director: Do you think it's possible that when many friends agree they might be wrong?

Friend: I do.

Director: And do you believe that when only a handful of friends agree they might be right?

Friend: Yes.

Director: So it's possible that few citizens might be better friends than many citizens?

Friend: Yes, it's possible.

Director: And would you rather be part of those who're right or those who're wrong?

Friend: Those who're right.

Director: But if those who're right are few, do you think they would sap the nation's strength? Didn't you say that a lack of friendship with the others does that?

Friend: I was wrong to say that. These few would be the core of the nation's strength.

Director: The core? How so?

Friend: The core is always that which is right. And these few are right about what's important. But they're not content to be right. They'll try to guide the many, to bring them into agreement, to make them friends. Then the nation would be truly strong.

Director: That sounds good, Friend. But what happens to those who just won't agree?

Friend: What happens to them? Why, nothing happens to them. Our nation is free, after all. And that means that just because you're not our friend, you don't have to be our enemy.

36 STATESMAN, POLITICIAN

Director: But what do you think the job of the statesman is?

Friend: To uphold the principles that make us free.

Director: What is the job of the mere politician?

Friend: His job is the same as that of the statesman, only he doesn't live up to it.

Director: What happens when he doesn't live up to it?

Friend: The opposite of freedom happens.

Director: Which is?

Friend: Slavery.

Director: Statesmen tend to make us free; politicians tend to make us slaves?

Friend: Exactly.

Director: To what do politicians make us slaves?

Friend: Our own vices, whatever they may be.

Director: And statesmen make us free through our virtues, by appealing to our virtues?

Friend: Yes.

Director: This appeal is the upholding of principles you mentioned?

Friend: That's right.

Director: And the opposite is the tearing down and trampling upon these principles?

Friend: You put that well.

Director: But what do you say to someone who says politicians and statesmen are not that powerful?

Friend: What do you mean?

Director: I mean, what if someone objects, saying that it's people who uphold or trample upon the principles they live by, not statesmen or politicians. After all, he'll say, virtue and vice are matters pertaining to the individual, not the state.

Friend: Is he denying that the condition of the state has an impact on our freedom?

Director: He'll want to know what that impact is.

Friend: All he'll have to do is look at a bad state, a tyranny, to see what sort of impact the condition of the state can have.

Director: Now here's the question he'll put. Which comes first? The corruption of the people or the corruption of the state?

Friend: I think it's a chicken and egg question. But let's say it's the people for the sake of argument.

Director: Alright. Now let's suppose there's a statesman upholding principles of freedom. It would still be possible for the people to become corrupt under his watch?

Friend: It would, and when they're fully corrupt they'd get rid of the statesman.

Director: And if there is a politician trampling principles of freedom, we're saying that the people must already be corrupt?

Friend: Yes.

Director: A corrupt people tends to bring corrupt leaders to power?

Friend: Right. If they were virtuous they would stop the corrupt from coming to power.

Director: And a virtuous people, a free people, tends to bring statesmen to power?

Friend: Agreed.

Director: So we're saying, essentially, that the people tend to get what they deserve?

Friend: Yes. But it doesn't always work that way.

Director: Why not? Do you believe that statesmen can arise among a corrupt people, or that politicians can appear among the virtuous?

Friend: Tell me what you think.

Director: Well, suppose a people is corrupt. Does that mean each and every individual among that people is corrupt?

Friend: No, of course not.

Director: But if the majority is corrupt and it's a democracy?

Friend: The state will likely be corrupt.

Director: But if it's only the minority that's corrupt and the majority is free?

Friend: A statesman can arise.

Director: Now, does a minority ever get its way?

Friend: It does, but it takes some luck.

Director: So a statesman might arise among a virtuous minority?

Friend: It's possible.

Director: And if the virtuous are in the majority, do they always elect statesmen to office?

Friend: Not necessarily, and for two reasons. One, no statesman might be available. Two, they might be fooled by one of the vicious.

Director: But they couldn't stay fooled for long, right? Wouldn't they simply vote him out once they come to know the truth?

Friend: Ideally, but vicious politicians often are good liars, are good at fooling the virtuous.

Director: In that case the virtuous people wouldn't get what they deserve?

Friend: That's right.

Director: And when a majority is corrupt, the minority of the virtuous generally doesn't get what it deserves, unless there is some luck that brings the statesman to power?

Friend: True.

Director: But when the majority is virtuous, and it gets what it deserves, which is a virtuous statesman, what does a vicious minority get?

Friend: It, too, gets what it deserves. Why? It's just punishment for the wicked to live under the virtuous and free. So when the virtuous get what they deserve, we all get what we deserve.

37 RESPECT

Director: What are manners?

Friend: Customary rules of conduct.

Director: Of what use are they?

Friend: They contribute to our freedom.

Director: How?

Friend: They ensure that we're treated with a certain amount of respect.

Director: Respect is an element of freedom?

Friend: Of course.

Director: Must we respect and be respected in turn, or is one or the other enough?

Friend: I think it must be both — respecting and being respected.

Director: And when we respect, do we respect those who are worthy of respect or those who are unworthy of respect?

Friend: Those who are worthy.

Director: How do we know who is worthy?

Friend: Those are worthy of respect who respect us.

Director: And in order for us to be respected we must be worthy of respect?

Friend: Naturally.

Director: And we're worthy of respect when we show respect to others?

Friend: Right.

Director: Now here's something I'm wondering. We said that as part of our freedom we must respect and be respected in turn. Yes?

Friend: Yes.

Director: So if someone treats us without respect that person takes away a part of our freedom?

Friend: True.

Director: Is there a way for us to get back that lost part of our freedom?

Friend: The only way is if that person comes to treat us with respect.

Director: But can't we simply remove ourselves from the presence of this person?

Friend: We can, in some cases.

Director: And, in those cases, we find others who respect us and then we respect them in turn, and thus we regain that lost bit of freedom?

Friend: I suppose.

Director: Now let me ask you this, Friend. Does respect only come from good manners, or are there other ways to get and give respect?

Friend: There are other ways.

Director: Do you think there can be a way of giving and getting respect that doesn't follow any rules, rules like those of good manners?

Friend: I think it's possible there can be.

Director: What would guide us in such a case?

Friend: Knowledge, not rules.

Director: Knowledge of what?

Friend: Knowledge of whether the other deserves respect.

Director: In the case of rules, manners, we said that someone deserves respect if he shows respect. Correct?

Friend: Correct.

Director: But this knowledge we're talking about now isn't based merely on the other showing respect?

Friend: It's not. A bad man can show you respect.

Director: And good manners would demand that you show the bad man respect in turn?

Friend: That's the problem with good manners. They don't discriminate.

Director: But the way of giving respect based on knowledge would dictate that you give no respect to a bad man, an evil man, regardless of how good his manners are?

Friend: That's right. They say the Devil is a gentleman, you know.

Director: So the knowledge we're talking of is a knowledge of good and evil?

Friend: Yes. You show respect only to the good.

Director: And you would care only for the respect of those who are good?

Friend: Right.

Director: What happens if you respect someone who is good but receive no respect in return? Do you think that such a case is possible?

Friend: I do, and it would be upsetting.

Director: Can you articulate why it would be upsetting?

Friend: Someone who's good, truly good, would show respect to someone who's good. If you receive no respect from someone good, that must mean that you're no good.

Director: But couldn't it be the case that you're mistaken, and that the person in question is in fact no good?

Friend: Sure, it's possible. But what if you get in the habit of thinking that only those who respect you are good? Can you see the danger? Can you see how arrogance might lead you down the wrong path? You'd think that anyone who doesn't respect you must be bad. But what if you're the one who's bad?

Director: I see the dilemma, Friend. So maybe it's better, after all, to have customary rules of conduct, manners, as opposed to conduct based simply on knowledge?

Friend: No, knowledge is better. We just have to make sure we really know both ourselves and others. Then we can respect, or not, with confidence.

Director: And in cases where we don't know ourselves or others?

Friend: We fall back on manners.

38 Courage

Friend: There is no freedom without courage.

Director: Why not?

Friend: Why not? Because it's scary being free.

Director: What makes it scary?

Friend: The choices you have to make.

Director: What's scary about choices?

Friend: The possible consequences of your choices.

Director: You're talking about bad consequences.

Friend: Of course.

Director: Are good consequences ever scary?

Friend: No.

Director: What do you need in order to make good choices?

Friend: Luck?

Director: Besides luck.

Friend: Knowledge and experience.

Director: You gain the knowledge from the experience?

Friend: Yes.

Director: So it would seem that it's important for someone who is to be free to start practicing making choices, gaining experience, at an early age, no?

Friend: I agree.

Director: Now, if you have the knowledge you need to make a good choice, meaning one with good consequences, would that choice be scary?

Friend: But how do you know for sure that you have the knowledge you need?

Director: For now let's just assume it's possible to know like that.

Friend: Okay, but you can know something and still be afraid to act on your knowledge.

Director: So knowledge is not a substitute for courage?

Friend: That's right.

Director: But if you know something and you're not afraid to act on your knowledge, do you still need courage? In other words, you only need courage when you're afraid?

Friend: I think that's true.

Director: Is a person who feels no fear free?

Friend: Well, in a certain sense he is.

Director: In what sense?

Friend: Not being afraid is a sort of freedom, a freedom from fear.

Director: But the courageous aren't free from fear.

Friend: No, they're not at all free from fear. The courageous are courageous precisely because they feel fear, and they overcome it.

Director: Now we have a problem.

Friend: What do you mean? What problem?

Director: We said there is no freedom without courage. Now we're saying there is no courage without fear. Do you see what this means?

Friend: There is no freedom without fear.

Director: Well, do you think that's true?

Friend: Of course I do. That's the whole point of what we've been saying. Like I said, it's scary making choices.

Director: What do you think of this choice?

Friend: What choice?

Director: What is the opposite of freedom?

Friend: Slavery.

Director: Do you have choices when you're a slave?

Friend: No, at least not like those you have when you're free.

Director: And if no choices, nothing scary?

Friend: True, as far as choices go.

Director: So when you're in slavery you have no fear, at least no fear like what you have when you're free, no fear coming from choices you have to make?

Friend: Yes, but what you do fear is the master. But what choice were you starting to ask me about? You haven't said.

Director: The choice of slavery over freedom, the choice that gets rid of the fear of choice, that gets rid of the need for courage. Do you think people ever make such a choice?

Friend: Do I think they do? People make that choice every day.

Director: How do they do this?

Friend: They let others make their choices for them.

Director: But is that really possible? Don't we all have to choose?

Friend: No, not all of us choose. We let others tell us what to do.

Director: Is this only when it comes to big, important things?

Friend: No, it's not. People are often slaves in the smallest, least important things. In fact, I think the little slavery prepares them for the big slavery.

Director: And there's nothing brave about a slave?

Friend: There can be — especially if the slave rebels against his master in hopes of being free.

Director: The attempt to become free would be scary?

Friend: Of course it would.

Director: So it would be like one of the difficult choices that the free must make?

Friend: Yes, and often times even more difficult.

Director: Then it seems that becoming free is excellent practice for being free.

39 REJECT

Director: Reject it. Push it away from you. That's how you'll stay free.

Friend: You really think it's that simple?

Director: Tell me why it isn't. You say you don't like the book.

Friend: But maybe I don't like it because I don't understand it. Maybe it can teach me something if I'm only willing to stick with it.

Director: Willing. That's what this is all about. You're willing yourself to read this book. You're not enjoying it. Now, I can see how if you had to read it for an assignment in school you might have to slog your way through it. But you're reading for pleasure — and not finding any pleasure.

Friend: But don't we need to do more than to read for pleasure? Shouldn't we also read to broaden our horizon?

Director: By broadening your horizon I suspect you mean being able to know what other people are talking about, when the book in question is popular. Is that so?

Friend: Well, don't you think that's important, to know what other people are talking about?

Director: But you can know what others are talking about by asking them about what they're talking about.

Friend: You mean to ask them to tell me more about the book, in depth?

Director: Yes. Then if what they say intrigues you, read the book. But if you start reading it, and give it at least something of a chance, a few chapters, say, and you find it doesn't interest you, doesn't intrigue you itself — then what's the point?

Friend: But like I said, maybe I just don't understand the book. Maybe I need to learn from it.

Director: Maybe the person who told you about the book doesn't understand what you understand. Have a little more confidence in your own judgment. Life's too short to go chasing down other people's tastes.

Friend: You really think I'll stay free by rejecting books that don't interest me?

Director: Yes. But then you have to find the books that do interest you.

Friend: But what if I don't find any?

Director: Have you never read an interesting book?

Friend: No, I have.

Director: Then use that as your starting point and keep branching out from there. Find books by the same author, find books that deal with related themes.

Friend: But what if I reject more books than I accept?

Director: I expect that would be the case — for someone with a taste that's pure.

Friend: But what if I go long stretches without finding anything new to read?

Director: That's easy. Re-read what you know you like until you find something new.

Friend: And that will keep me free?

Director: Yes. Your spirit won't be chained to things you don't actually care for. Tell me, Friend. When you force yourself to work your way through something you don't like, what do you feel?

Friend: I feel dread.

Director: And yet you feel compelled to keep going?

Friend: Like I said, maybe I just don't get it. After all, we're talking about famous books — classics, even. How can you reject classics?

Director: By simply closing the books and setting them aside. Reject them.

Friend: You make it sound like rejecting is an exercise of power.

Director: It is. And it's an exercise of power when you find and read books that make you feel free.

Friend: What is it about a book that makes you feel free, exactly?

Director: What is it about anything that makes you feel free?

Friend: I think it's self-affirmation.

Director: And what would make you feel un-free?

Friend: The opposite — denial of myself.

Director: Which means not being true to yourself?

Friend: That's exactly what it means.

Director: And certain books aren't true to you?

Friend: I suppose that's true.

Director: While other books are in fact true to you?

Friend: Yes, certain books are.

Director: And you will learn about yourself, or re-affirm what you already know, in the course of reading these books?

Friend: Yes.

Director: And in the books you ought to reject you can feel that you have nothing to learn, or re-affirm, about yourself?

Friend: I agree, Director. But this somehow seems wrong.

Director: It's wrong to reject books that don't speak to you about yourself?

Friend: But they can speak to me about others.

Director: Others that aren't like you?

Friend: Yes.

Director: Well, what would you like to know about these others who aren't like you?

Friend: I'd like to know what they're like.

Director: And you have to read their books to know that?

Friend: Well, I suppose I could talk to them, right? Ask them questions about themselves?

Director: Yes, that's true.

Friend: But there's a problem.

Director: What problem?

Friend: It takes more courage to talk than read — and I'm not always very brave.

40 AUTHORITY

Friend: Do you think we can ever be free of authority?

Director: Why would we want to be?

Friend: Because authority is oppressive.

Director: Do you believe it's always oppressive?

Friend: Yes, in varying degrees.

Director: Is it oppressive even when it helps you?

Friend: When does it help you? It just tells you what to do.

Director: Can't it help you if it tells you to do something that's good for you?

Friend: But I already know what's good for me. I don't need authority to tell me that.

Director: If both you and authority know what's good for you, what harm is there in a little reminder from authority?

Friend: But doesn't that little reminder amount to my not being free?

Director: Because you're free only when you freely choose what you do, without being told?

Friend: Of course.

Director: And it's better to choose freely than to be told, even if you make a bad choice?

Friend: Yes.

Director: Well, then it's a good thing.

Friend: What's a good thing?

Director: It's a good thing that you're free to listen to authority or not.

Friend: But if I don't listen I have to pay the price.

Director: Don't all choices involve a price?

Friend: Yes, but not listening to authority often comes at a very steep price.

Director: Then maybe the only time you don't listen is when authority tells you to do something that's bad for you, something that comes at a higher cost than not listening.

Friend: I agree.

Director: Let's explore this a bit further. Do you agree that an authority that tells us to do something that's bad for us is a bad authority?

Friend: Certainly.

Director: And is bad authority false authority? Or should we call it true authority?

Friend: It's false authority.

Director: False because such authority presents itself as good for us but really isn't? Or do you think false authority comes right out and says to do something because it's bad for us?

Friend: No, false authority pretends to be telling us to do something that's good for us.

Director: Does it follow that true authority tells us to do something that's actually good for us?

Friend: It follows.

Director: But we don't want to be told what to do, even if it's something good.

Friend: No, we don't.

Director: So what if true authority, instead of telling us what to do, tries to persuade us?

Friend: Persuade? But then what would make it an authority? Authority tells us what to do.

Director: But what if it only tells us to do what we think is reasonable?

Friend: Then it's being reasonable that makes true authority an authority.

Director: Yes. But there's a difficulty.

Friend: What difficulty?

Director: I'll try to explain. What do we need in order to determine what's reasonable?

Friend: We need the facts.

Director: Where do we get the facts?

Friend: Sometimes we can find them out ourselves.

Director: But when we can't?

Friend: Authority supplies them.

Director: And if we get our facts from authority, what do we have to do?

Friend: We have to check those facts.

Director: Do we check them ourselves?

Friend: Ideally. But that's not always possible.

Director: Who checks the facts then? No one?

Friend: Of course not. The facts must be checked by someone.

Director: Someone who's an authority on the facts in question?

Friend: Well, yes.

Director: And this authority will tell us what to think about these facts?

Friend: I suppose.

Director: Do you see why I said there's a difficulty?

Friend: Yes. If we don't like an authority that tells us what to do, how much do we like an authority that tells us what to think?

Director: Is one authority preferable to the other?

Friend: If the one that tells us what to think has to persuade us, and the one that tells us what to do doesn't, then I prefer the one that tells us what to think.

Director: And if that authority on what to think doesn't persuade us?

Friend: We won't listen.

Director: We said not listening to authority comes at a price. What kind of price will we have to pay if we don't listen to an authority on facts?

Friend: It depends on the facts in question. I mean, what if we don't listen to a true authority on nuclear safety? We might pay a very steep price. So I guess we have to hope that such authorities speak persuasively — and that we're open to persuasion when they do.

41 SELF-CONTROL

Director: What's the one thing you need when you're free?

Friend: Self-control.

Director: Why?

Friend: If you lack self-control, and you're free, you'll just run amok.

Director: So no one should be free who lacks self-control?

Friend: Right. If freedom is the right, self-control is the responsibility.

Director: What is self-control?

Friend: It's making sure you don't harm yourself or others in the exercise of your freedom.

Director: So you have to know what harm is, to either yourself or others?

Friend: You do.

Director: Well, how do you know when you're harming others?

Friend: In some cases it is obvious. In others you have to know the person in question pretty well.

Director: So if you punch someone in the nose, you know you're harming him? But if you say something somewhat insensitive and hurt his feelings, you might not know you're harming him?

Friend: Yes, but it's more complicated than that. Suppose you punch someone in the nose while trying to prevent him from driving drunk. Are you really harming or protecting him and others? As for hurt feelings, at times you know full well if you're hurting someone that way or not. And at times you may have to bruise his feelings to tell him an important truth that will serve him well in the future.

Director: So the causing of pain alone does not necessarily make for harm?

Friend: Correct.

Director: The pain must be for a greater purpose than the simple causing of pain?

Friend: That's right.

Director: Then as far as self-control is concerned, we can be exercising it while inflicting others with pain, awful as that may sound.

Friend: Yes.

Director: And we need to be controlled because it's possible to go too far?

Friend: Of course.

Director: So self-control is, basically, knowing how much is enough and acting on that knowledge.

Friend: Certainly.

Director: It's like that when we eat or drink, isn't it? I mean, we have to know when enough food or drink is truly enough.

Friend: Yes, we do.

Director: How do we know when we've had enough to eat or drink?

Friend: We can feel it when we have.

Director: And how do we know when we've used enough force in order to stop someone who wants to drive drunk?

Friend: When we succeed in stopping him.

Director: So if he struggles against us we simply use more force on him until he stops?

Friend: Yes.

Director: But then where is the self-control?

Friend: It comes in using only the minimum amount of force necessary.

Director: Is that the way it is with food and drink? We eat and drink the minimum amount necessary to satisfy our hunger and quench our thirst?

Friend: I suppose it is.

Director: So self-control amounts to knowing what the minimum is?

Friend: Yes.

Director: But couldn't self-control also be knowing what the maximum is? I mean, suppose you really like a certain dish of food. You want to eat more than the bare minimum of what will satisfy your hunger. Is there a maximum amount you can eat that won't be too much but will be more than barely enough?

Friend: There is.

Director: And it's the same with drink? You want more than just the bare minimum to quench your thirst but you don't want to become drunk?

Friend: Yes.

Director: So it seems that self-control in some cases is about the minimum, and in some cases is about the maximum. Might that mean there can be a range of self-control between minimum and maximum? Or is there only a single, optimal point of self-control, with a shade too far on either side of it being too little or too much?

Friend: I think there's a range of self-control.

Director: Now, we said that self-control concerns both ourselves and others. And we talked about harm to others. Right?

Friend: But I think we also touched on harm to ourselves when we talked about food and drink. Too much food or drink can be harmful.

Director: That's true. But fortunately we can, for the most part, feel when enough is enough. But now I'm wondering something, Friend.

Friend: What?

Director: We said there's a range of self-control. Doesn't that mean there are many possible points at which we'll feel we've had enough?

Friend: Yes. This isn't a perfect science. There's no one ideal point at which to stop.

Director: But aren't there clear lines on either end of the range? They divide not enough from enough, and enough from too much. Or is everything a bit more gray than that?

Friend: No, there are lines. If you feel sick from eating, it's clear you've crossed the line dividing enough from too much.

Director: And if you fail to cross the first line, the line dividing not enough from enough?

Friend: Then I guess you starve.

42 WHAT OTHERS THINK

Director: Does what others think matter, Friend?

Friend: Of course it does.

Director: How so?

Friend: What others think affects your life.

Director: Can you give me an example?

Friend: Sure. What your boss thinks about you can determine whether you get a raise in pay or not.

Director: I thought that the quality of my work determines that.

Friend: Your work, you — what's the difference?

Director: What if the boss isn't a good judge of the quality of my work? Does that mean he isn't a good judge of who I am?

Friend: Well, he can judge you to be a good person but not like your work.

Director: And he might like my work but judge me to be a bad person?

Friend: Yes.

Director: What if he doesn't like my work but I do? Should I change my work in order to please him?

Friend: It's hard to say, Director.

Director: Why?

Friend: I guess it has to do with why you're working.

Director: What do you mean?

Friend: I mean, you might simply be working in order to make a living. If that's the case, then I'd say you should change your work to please the boss.

Director: And when would I not change my work?

Friend: When you love your work.

Director: And if I love my work I should be free to perform it any way I see fit?

Friend: Ideally, yes.

Director: Do you believe it's possible for me to love my work yet not be very good at it?

Friend: I suppose so.

Director: In that case, if the boss criticizes it justly, should I listen?

Friend: Of course you should. You want to improve.

Director: But if the boss criticizes my work unjustly, I shouldn't listen?

Friend: That's right — up to a point.

Director: What point?

Friend: The point where it will cost you your job.

Director: And this is how it is with other people, too?

Friend: What do you mean?

Director: As concerns my true work, I can only not listen to others up to a point?

Friend: What work are you referring to, Director — philosophy?

Director: Yes.

Friend: Well, don't you think for philosophy you have to care what others think?

Director: Can you give me an example?

Friend: Your friends. You want them to think highly of what you do, don't you?

Director: I'd like them to appreciate my work.

Friend: And when you talk with them, when you philosophize, what do you do?

Director: We examine our opinions together.

Friend: An opinion is what someone thinks, right?

Director: True enough.

Friend: So that goes to show that you do in fact care what your friends think.

Director: A point well made and taken. But does what a friend thinks change the way I go about my work?

Friend: You're asking whether your method is the same no matter to whom you are speaking?

Director: What do you think?

Friend: From what I've observed your method is the same.

Director: And wouldn't that mean, in a way, that I don't care what people think?

Friend: So you care what people think as far as their opinions go, but don't care what people think as it concerns your approach?

Director: Well, the word "approach" makes me have second thoughts.

Friend: Why?

Director: Sometimes when you want to get at an opinion, to bring it out to the light of day, there is a thicket of other things you must make your way through before you get to that opinion. The approach varies depending on the nature of the obstacles.

Friend: How thick the thicket is.

Director: Yes.

Friend: So you change your tactics, not your strategy.

Director: I suppose that's true. But what's the strategy?

Friend: You mean you don't know? It's to bring people to the truth.

Director: But isn't that a goal, not a strategy?

Friend: Surely you know what your strategy is, Director.

Director: Maybe the strategy is to bring opinions out into the light of day, in order to help us toward our goal, the truth, by means of various approaches, or tactics, depending on conditions.

Friend: That sounds like a fine plan to me. Don't let anyone talk you out of it.

Director: I won't hear a word against it.

43 FRIENDS

Director: Can people who are free be friends with those who are slaves?

Friend: You mean people who actually are slaves, as in forced servitude, or people who simply act slavishly?

Director: People who act slavishly.

Friend: Why would the free want to be friends with them?

Director: You think a friendship between the two types is unlikely?

Friend: Yes, very. In fact, I don't even know if it's possible. Sure, they can say they are friends and be on a friendly basis. But they won't truly be friends.

Director: Why is that?

Friend: Because real friendship is based on mutual admiration. What can the free admire in those who're slaves?

Director: What do the free admire in their friends?

Friend: Truthfulness, for one.

Director: And slaves aren't truthful?

Friend: Of course they're not. They hide the truth about themselves, especially about what they think, from both themselves and others.

Director: The free don't want to hide anything, from either themselves or others?

Friend: First and foremost, the free hide nothing from themselves. They are honest with themselves. And when it comes to sharing what they think with others, they exercise caution, but they share.

Director: And what about the slaves? What do they share?

Friend: You mean when they're not lying? The only thing they have to share — their doubts and fears.

Director: Do you think it's excessive doubt and fear that makes them slaves in the first place?

Friend: I think that's a big part of it.

Director: The free are more certain and more brave than the slaves?

Friend: Of course they are.

Director: Do you think the doubts and fears of the slaves would bring the free people down if they were to become friends?

Friend: An occasional doubt or fear is fine — it's only human. But constant cringing and sniveling makes for bad company to someone more or less free of all that. So yes, they would bring the free people down.

Director: But what if a slave stands up to his doubts and his fears? What if he uses his doubt as the basis for hunting the truth? What if he is brave in the hunt?

Friend: You sound like you're talking about a philosopher.

Director: Well, what if I am? Is the philosopher a slave?

Friend: Of course he isn't.

Director: Then he is free?

Friend: Certainly.

Director: With whom can he be friends? Would the free have him?

Friend: The truly free would.

Director: What's the difference between the truly free and the merely free?

Friend: The truly free aren't afraid of the questions a philosopher would ask.

Director: It's part of their not wanting to hide what they think, right?

Friend: Right.

Director: Does that mean the merely free hide what they think? Does that make them like the slaves?

Friend: Let's just say there are degrees of truthfulness.

Director: And slaves are the least truthful?

Friend: Yes.

Director. So a philosopher, if he's one who loves the truth, would be likely to be friends most of all with the truly free, then with the merely free, and then with the slaves?

Friend: But why would the philosopher want to be friends with the slaves?

Director: Because it seems they have something in common with the philosopher.

Friend: What?

Director: Their doubts. The difference is that they just lack the courage to try and clear them up.

Friend: Do you think a philosopher can teach the slavish to be brave?

Director: Maybe it's possible to teach some of them what's not to be feared. Don't you think that amounts to much the same thing?

Friend: I do. But then what happens?

Director: What do you mean?

Friend: If these slaves aren't afraid to clear up their doubts, and do in fact clear up their doubts, does that make them... free?

Director: What do you think?

Friend: I suppose it does, if they really have an interest in truth now.

Director: And if they do, then it's no more cringing and sniveling?

Friend: No, none of that.

Director: And if there's none of that, if they're free, with a full interest in truth — then might these former slaves become the friends of those who're free?

Friend: Yes.

Director: The free wouldn't turn them away?

Friend: Why would they? Not only will they admire these former slaves for being free, they'll admire them for having overcome slavery.

Director: But is that all a former slave must overcome if he's to be friends with the free?

Friend: Well, no. I think there's one more thing. He must overcome his shame for having been a slave. And that can be every bit as hard as overcoming the slavery itself.

44 POTENTIAL

Director: Who has the potential to be free?

Friend: Anyone who can think for himself.

Director: And what does thinking for yourself mean?

Friend: It means listening to your own voice, and only your own voice.

Director: But how can that be? Are we to live isolated in a cave? Don't we have to listen to the voices of others?

Friend: Sure, but then we go off on our own and think on our own, with our own voice, our own words.

Director: Our own words? Aren't words shared by everyone who speaks the language?

Friend: You can make words your own.

Director: How?

Friend: By knowing, really knowing, what they mean.

Director: But what does it mean to know a word?

Friend: It means to have that word correspond to something in you that is more than mere words.

Director: Do you mean that your words must have a place in your heart?

Friend: Yes.

Director: And when you speak these words to yourself, you are speaking from the heart?

Friend: You are.

Director: And this is thinking?

Friend: I think it is.

Director: If you speak freely to yourself from the heart, are you free?

Friend: I believe you are.

Director: Do you think there is more to freedom than that, or is that all that freedom is?

Friend: Well, you have to speak to others.

Director: Do you speak to them from the heart?

Friend: You do.

Director: And when you speak from the heart to others, you're free?

Friend: Yes.

Director: Is there ever a time when you can't speak to yourself from the heart?

Friend: No, there shouldn't be.

Director: But what about when you're speaking to others?

Friend: That's the harder case. I like to think you should always be free to speak from the heart. But I don't think it's always possible.

Director: Why wouldn't it be?

Friend: Sometimes you have to lie.

Director: You have to lie, or you choose to lie?

Friend: Sometimes you choose to lie, sometimes you have to lie.

Director: Are you free in either case?

Friend: No, you're not.

Director: If you have to lie, I suppose there's no helping it. But would you ever really choose to lie? That would mean choosing not to be free, if what we've been saying is correct.

Friend: You're right — it would be choosing not to be free.

Director: I'm not sure that's possible.

Friend: Why not?

Director: What could be more important than being free?

Friend: I'm not sure.

Director: If nothing is more important than being free, it would never make sense not to speak from the heart, not to be free.

Friend: But we said sometimes you don't have a choice.

Director: You mean like if someone has a gun to your head?

Friend: Exactly.

Director: Well, in that case someone has already taken your freedom from you. But now that I've said that, I'm not sure it's true.

Friend: What do you mean?

Director: I mean, can anyone ever really take your freedom from you? Even in the case of the gun, can't you find a way, some way, to stand up for your freedom?

Friend: Not everyone is that brave, Director.

Director: But should they be?

Friend: Ideally, yes.

Director: If someone doesn't stand up, if someone surrenders, what does it say?

Friend: It says that something else is more important than freedom.

Director: In this case, what would that most likely be?

Friend: Mere life.

Director: Do you think that mere life is more important than freedom?

Friend: No. But I'm not sure I'd be able to stand up to the gun.

Director: I wonder if that's because you only believe that freedom is the most important thing.

Friend: What do you mean?

Director: Don't you have to know, truly know, that freedom is the most important thing — not just believe?

Friend: But what's the difference between believing and knowing?

Director: In this case? All the difference in the world.

45 ESCAPE

Director: When you escape from something are you free?

Friend: I suppose it depends what you escape from. For instance, if you escape from prison you're free in one sense. But in another sense, the sense in which you're a fugitive, you can't possibly be free.

Director: Why can't fugitives be free?

Friend: Because they're always fearful of being caught and brought back to prison.

Director: And is everyone who escapes from something fearful of being caught?

Friend: I wouldn't say everyone is.

Director: Can you give me an example of someone who isn't?

Friend: Sure — someone who escapes from ignorance.

Director: Can ignorance be like a prison?

Friend: Like a prison? Ignorance is a prison, a very real prison.

Director: And how do you escape from this prison?

Friend: Why, through knowledge.

Director: And if you gain in knowledge and free yourself from ignorance, no one will come after you to catch you and bring you back to the prison of the mind?

Friend: It doesn't work like that. Sure, people might resent your new found knowledge, and that can make things difficult for you. But I believe that once you have knowledge it can't be taken away from you — for any knowledge that really counts, that is.

Director: You mean you might forget something you know that isn't very important?

Friend: Exactly.

Director: But truly important things you can never forget?

Friend: No, you can't.

Director: Tell me, Friend. Do you believe you have to live up to what you know?

Friend: Of course I do.

Director: So if you escape from the prison of the mind through knowledge, then fail to live up to that knowledge, what happens?

Friend: You're imprisoned once more.

Director: In what?

Friend: The prison of cowardice.

Director: And how does one escape from the prison of cowardice?

Friend: Simply through courage — through being brave enough to live up to what you know.

Director: Now, we've mentioned three sorts of prisons — prison for the body, prison for the mind, and prison for... what?

Friend: The soul. Courage is a matter of soul.

Director: If we escape from the prison of the soul, we're truly free?

Friend: We are.

Director: And what if we escape from the prison of the mind — are we truly free?

Friend: Only as long as we live up to what we know.

Director: And if we merely escape from the prison of the body?

Friend: We're not truly free.

Director: Because we live in fear of being caught and returned to prison.

Friend: That's what we said.

Director: Does it matter whether you actually committed the crime for which you were imprisoned?

Friend: Of course it does.

Director: But regardless of whether you are truly innocent or guilty, when you escape you still aren't really free?

Friend: No, you're not.

Director: Then how are you ever free of the prison of the body?

Friend: You serve your term and are released.

Director: If you were unjustly convicted, does that seem fair?

Friend: Of course it doesn't, no.

Director: So, just to be clear, are we saying, essentially, that there is no true escape from an unjust conviction, assuming all appeals are exhausted and so on?

Friend: Yes, but I don't like the way that sounds.

Director: Well, maybe something that we've said leading up to this point isn't right.

Friend: What?

Director: That you would worry endlessly about being caught and returned to prison.

Friend: But you would worry endlessly about that.

Director: Would this worry do you any good?

Friend: It might make you more cautious and therefore more safe.

Director: But can't you take precautions without worrying?

Friend: I suppose you can.

Director: In that case worry would do no good?

Friend: True.

Director: Then that would be the first step — knowing that worry does no good. What step do you think is next?

Friend: I know what step is next — living up to that knowledge and letting go of worry.

Director: So not only do you have to free your body, but you have to free your mind and soul. And if you accomplish this triple feat of freedom, you would be free in the full sense of the word, though a fugitive?

Friend: But only if you're truly innocent. Then you have a clear conscience.

Director: I see. That's another sort of freedom, the fourth that goes into the escape?

Friend: It is. And without it, the other three aren't worth a thing.

46 Ignorance

Director: Can ignorance ever make you free, Friend?

Friend: Well, they say ignorance is bliss, you know.

Director: Are freedom and bliss one and the same?

Friend: No, of course they're not.

Director: Which would you rather have, freedom or bliss?

Friend: Freedom.

Director: Why?

Friend: Bliss is fleeting.

Director: And what is freedom?

Friend: Enduring.

Director: Is freedom a thing you know firsthand?

Friend: It is.

Director: Then you would know to what extent ignorance plays a part in your freedom.

Friend: I would, and I do. It doesn't play any part whatsoever in my freedom.

Director: Let's see if that's true. Can you be ignorant of what it feels like to do a certain good thing?

Friend: Of course. You've just never done that certain good thing.

Director: Does this have any bearing on your freedom?

Friend: No, it doesn't. Say it's good to adopt a cat from a shelter. You might never have adopted a cat, so you're ignorant of what it feels like to do so. But you can, in your ignorance, still be free. It seems silly even to have to spell this out.

Director: What happens if we push this out a bit further? Suppose you're ignorant of what it feels like to do anything good.

Friend: You mean you've never done a good deed?

Director: Yes. Oh, I know it may seem unlikely. But it's possible, isn't it?

Friend: Yes, I suppose it is.

Director: So let's assume you're in complete ignorance of what it feels like to do a good deed, any good deed. Under those circumstances, can you still be free?

Friend: It sounds terrible to say, but yes — I believe you can. Part of true freedom is being able to choose what you do, and what you don't do. No one can force you to do a good deed.

Director: Now let's turn things around and see what we see. Does what we've been saying hold for bad things as well?

Friend: You mean can you be completely ignorant of how it feels to do a certain bad thing and still be free? Of course you can.

Director: And is it possible to be free if you're completely ignorant of how it feels to do any bad thing at all?

Friend: Yes, unlikely as that may be.

Director: So, to sum things up, we can say that a certain sort of ignorance, ignorance of how it feels to do either something good or bad, does not prevent one from being free.

Friend: Yes.

Director: Now that we've established that, do you know what we must turn to next?

Friend: I don't.

Director: We must question whether a certain amount of ignorance not only is not harmful to, but is in fact a necessary component of, freedom.

Friend: I'll be surprised if we find that to be so.

Director: Let's start with something simple. What is the opposite of ignorance?

Friend: Knowledge.

Director: If you have knowledge of how it feels to do a certain good deed, does that negatively affect your freedom?

Friend: Of course not.

Director: But what if you have knowledge of how it feels to do a certain bad deed?

Friend: No one's perfect. We all have knowledge of how it feels to do bad deeds.

Director: Ah, but are all bad deeds the same as far as this knowledge and its effect on freedom goes?

Friend: I'm not following.

Director: Is a lie a bad deed?

Friend: Of course it is, generally speaking.

Director: If you have knowledge of how it feels to lie, you can still be free?

Friend: No one would be free if that weren't true.

Director: Now how about if you set fire to your neighbor's house for no good reason?

Friend: That's a different sort of thing.

Director: If you have knowledge of how it feels to do that, can you still be free? Can you see how far we can take this, on and on through bad deed after bad deed?

Friend: I can see where this leads. The ultimate question is whether someone who has complete knowledge of how it feels to commit all crimes can be free, right?

Director: And what do you think?

Friend: I think the weight of these deeds would crush his freedom.

Director: And ignorance of what it feels like to commit these deeds is the only way to keep that weight from growing too great for him to carry?

Friend: I think that's true.

Director: Then you know what our discussion seems to indicate, don't you?

Friend: I do. A certain sort of ignorance can keep you free.

Director: Shall we give a name to this certain sort of ignorance, or should we just call it a certain sort?

Friend: We should give it a name. And the name is innocence.

47 TOLERANCE, RESPECT

Director: Can you be free without being tolerant of others?

Friend: Yes, I think you can. I know it sounds bad, but it's true.

Director: Can you be free if others don't tolerate you?

Friend: No, you can't.

Director: So if everyone hopes to be free without tolerating others, no one will be free?

Friend: Yes.

Director: If you're tolerant will you automatically be tolerated in turn?

Friend: No, I don't think it works that way.

Director: And if you're tolerated will you automatically be free?

Friend: No. There's more to freedom than that.

Director: What more does it take to be free than to be tolerated?

Friend: Respect.

Director: You need respect in order to be free?

Friend: Don't you think you do?

Director: Let's assume you do. Whose respect do you need?

Friend: What do you mean?

Director: I mean, do you need the respect of an ignoramus in order to be free?

Friend: Of course not.

Director: Well, what if it's an ignoramus who respects whatever it is you're doing?

Friend: That doesn't matter. I want the respect of someone who knows.

Director: Knows what?

Friend: Knows that what I am doing is worthy of respect.

Director: And what might you be doing that deserves both tolerance and respect?

Friend: It could be any number of things.

Director: I see. Now here's something I'm wondering. Is there ever a time when something that's respected isn't tolerated?

Friend: No. I think we always tolerate that which we respect.

Director: So if you can secure respect, that's enough?

Friend: Yes.

Director: You know what follows then, don't you?

Friend: I do. The only time you need tolerance is when what you're doing isn't respected, when you're not respected.

Director: What's easier to secure, tolerance or respect?

Friend: I'd say it's tolerance.

Director: So you should seek to be tolerated first and then hope to come to be respected?

Friend: That make sense. But....

Director: But?

Friend: To merely be tolerated is to be contemptible in the eyes of the one who tolerates you.

Director: Do you really think that all those who merely tolerate something do so with contempt?

Friend: Don't you?

Director: I think that tolerance can be a matter of simple indifference, if not principle.

Friend: But I don't want people to be indifferent toward me.

Director: You'd rather they have contempt for you?

Friend: Of course not. I'd rather earn their respect.

Director: Well, what's the difference between tolerance and respect?

Friend: The only criterion for tolerance is that you don't think the thing in question will cause you any harm.

Director: The things you think are respectable, do you think they will cause you any harm?

Friend: Of course not. You think they are difficult and worth doing.

Director: Is it possible for something difficult to be harmful to you?

Friend: I suppose it is.

Director: So difficulty by itself can't tell us whether something is respectable.

Friend: Right. It's as I said. The thing must also be worth doing.

Director: And what's worth doing?

Friend: Something that's beneficial.

Director: And the beneficial, if difficult, is always respected?

Friend: If people know it's difficult and beneficial, then yes.

Director: The knowing is the thing, as far as respect is concerned?

Friend: It is.

Director: Where do we get the knowledge we need in order to respect properly?

Friend: From experience. From life.

Director: Are you saying we have to gain this knowledge all on our own?

Friend: I am.

Director: You don't believe it can be taught?

Friend: I don't think we can teach this knowledge, Director.

Director: But why?

Friend: Because the ones in need of teaching won't tolerate our trying to teach them.

Director: They think what we're teaching is harmful?

Friend: They generally just think it's annoying. But annoyance, for some, is enough.

48 DEMAGOGUES

Friend: I'm sick of all the demagogues who would steal our freedom.

Director: And so am I. But I'm not sure what you mean by demagogue.

Friend: I mean what everyone means — a leader who plays on popular prejudices and makes false claims and promises in order to come to power.

Director: And he comes to power in hopes of stealing our freedom?

Friend: I think he only cares about coming to power. The stealing of freedom is something that simply follows from our allowing him to come to power.

Director: So freedom requires that we not decide who is to rule based upon our prejudices?

Friend: That's right.

Director: Then we must decide based upon knowledge?

Friend: Freedom requires that we do.

Director: And what about the false claims that the demagogue makes?

Friend: Freedom demands that we know enough to see that the claims are in fact false.

Director: What about the false promises? Is it the same with them?

Friend: Yes, we have to see through these empty pledges.

Director: And we see through them by means of knowledge?

Friend: Well, these things are a little harder to know about — but yes.

Director: So, in every case, the demagogue can be defeated by knowledge?

Friend: I think that's true.

Director: Is knowledge always enough to prevent anyone from stealing our freedom?

Friend: Well, there are two sorts of enemy to freedom — internal and external. Knowledge protects us from the internal.

Director: Assuming we act on that knowledge.

Friend: Of course.

Director: And what of the external enemies to freedom?

Friend: We need strength to overcome them.

Director: By strength you mean force?

Friend: Yes, force.

Director: Assuming we can't deter the enemy, we must employ this force?

Friend: We must.

Director: Now, perhaps you'll think I'm being tedious, but don't we need knowledge of when and how to employ our force?

Friend: No, you're not being tedious. We do need this knowledge.

Director: If demagogues are in power among us internally, how likely is it that those in charge will have the knowledge needed to employ our force properly externally?

Friend: I don't think it's very likely.

Director: But if we can overcome popular prejudices, false claims, and false promises, it's more likely that we'll have the knowledge we need?

Friend: Yes, both internally and externally.

Director: Because both foreign and domestic policy depend on knowledge?

Friend: Yes, to be sure.

Director: Then tell me this, Friend. If a demagogue depends on popular prejudices, and he comes to power — what does this mean?

Friend: It must mean that those with prejudices, rather than those with knowledge, are in the majority.

Director: Do you think it's possible to eradicate prejudice?

Friend: No, I don't — not completely, at least.

Director: Do you think there are many sorts of prejudice?

Friend: I do.

Director: What sort of prejudice do demagogues rely upon?

Friend: Political prejudice.

Director: Do you think it's possible to get rid of political prejudice?

Friend: I think that is the worst sort of prejudice, the hardest to do away with.

Director: Why?

Friend: Because, ultimately, it's about how we live.

Director: Then tell me. What makes a people free?

Friend: You mean as far as their leaders go? The opposite of demagogues being in power.

Director: What's the opposite of a demagogue?

Friend: A true leader.

Director: You said we can't eradicate prejudices. How does a true leader deal with them?

Friend: He confronts them.

Director: And?

Friend: He hopes that there are enough people without prejudice who will see what he is doing and will support him.

Director: So, as far as the leader is concerned, everything depends upon his supporters — in particular the quality of their minds, what they know?

Friend: Yes. But he can't exactly go around talking about the quality of people's minds.

Director: Why not? Isn't it precisely the best kind of leader who will? He'll make a direct appeal to their knowledge.

Friend: And a demagogue will make a direct appeal to what people think they know.

Director: Are you afraid that more people think they know than actually know?

Friend: Afraid? That's how we got into this mess in the first place.

Director: If that's true, then it seems we've got our first clue as to how we get out.

49 BORN

Director: What does it mean to be born free?

Friend: It means to be born into circumstances that make you free.

Director: You mean like being born in a certain country?

Friend: Sure.

Director: Is that all it takes to be free, to be born in a certain country?

Friend: Maybe it's better to say that being born in a certain country gives you the opportunity to be free.

Director: Because freedom is something you have to live up to?

Friend: Yes.

Director: But not everyone lives up to being free given the chance?

Friend: That's right.

Director: Those who do live up to being free, how do they do this?

Friend: They hold to the values of the free.

Director: And in a free country the values of the country are the values of the free?

Friend: They are.

Director: Well, what about those who live in free countries but aren't free?

Friend: What about them?

Director: What prevents them from holding to the values of the free?

Friend: On the one hand, nothing.

Director: But on the other hand?

Friend: Their circumstances.

Director: Their circumstances?

Friend: Yes, the environment they're born into.

Director: But isn't their country their environment?

Friend: It is.

Director: Then what are you talking about?

Friend: Something that's an even bigger influence on you than the country of your birth.

Director: But what could that be?

Friend: Your family.

Director: And your family can prevent you from holding to the values of the free?

Friend: Yes, your family circumstances can overwhelm you.

Director: But how?

Friend: Your family might not live up to the values of the country.

Director: And if it doesn't, you're doomed not to live up to them, too?

Friend: You're not necessarily doomed. But you have a very serious obstacle to overcome.

Director: But in a free country, how likely is it that everyone in your family, every single person, would fail to adopt free values?

Friend: Oh, you might be surprised.

Director: But really, Friend. Even if there is only one person in your family — in the farthest extension of your family — who does adopt free values, couldn't you learn from that person?

Friend: You could. But there are two people who count most in your family.

Director: Let me guess. Your father and your mother?

Friend: Of course.

Director: So if you are born into a life where either one of these, or both, don't live up to the values of the country, the free country, you're saying that you will have a hard time living up to those values yourself?

Friend: Yes.

Director: Then you're saying, essentially, that for some it's harder to be free than for others, despite all being born equally into a free country?

Friend: Don't you agree?

Director: I'm not so sure. It seems to me that a bit of adversity early in life can go a long way in later years.

Friend: If you succeed in overcoming the adversity.

Director: Yes. But tell me, Friend. If you were fed the values of freedom with your mother's milk, as it were, how hard do you think it would be for you to be free, to be truly free?

Friend: Relatively speaking? I don't think it would be as hard.

Director: But is that really true?

Friend: Why wouldn't it be? You were raised to be free.

Director: What does it mean to be raised? To be taught?

Friend: Yes.

Director: Well, aren't being taught to be free and actually being free two very different things? Don't you have to do something on your own in order to be free? Or is it enough simply to be taught?

Friend: No, it's not enough. You have to learn what you're being taught.

Director: And not everyone learns what he's taught, regardless if it's his parents, some other, or simply life itself doing the teaching?

Friend: True.

Director: Could that be because the lessons of freedom aren't easy to learn?

Friend: I don't think they're easy to learn, Director.

Director: And if learning the lessons is hard, no matter their source, how hard do you think it is to act on what you've learned?

Friend: It's even harder.

Director: Then learn all you can and act on what you learn, Friend. And know that not even those who seem to be born free, with every advantage, can take freedom for granted.

50 Want

Director: What is freedom?

Friend: Being able to do what you want.

Director: I hope you won't find me tedious if I ask you whether being able to do what you want is enough. After all, can't you be able to do something but not do it?

Friend: But why would you not do what you want to do if you're able to do it?

Director: That's a good question. Maybe we can think of an example.

Friend: Hmm. How about this? You want to tell your boss off. You're able to tell him off. But you don't.

Director: But are you really able to tell him off?

Friend: Of course you are. You just don't want the consequences that will likely follow from telling him off.

Director: Bad consequences don't affect your ability to do something?

Friend: Right. We're able to jump off of a bridge despite the bad consequences that follow.

Director: And you believe that being able to do something is enough, that being able makes us free?

Friend: I do.

Director: I don't know, Friend. In that case slaves, real and literal slaves, would be free just because they're able to stop working any time they like. They might be beaten and whipped for doing so, but they're able to do it nonetheless.

Friend: Well, that doesn't sound so good as far as freedom goes.

Director: Maybe we have to qualify your definition of freedom.

Friend: How?

Director: By saying that freedom is being able to do what you want without the likelihood of bad consequences.

Friend: But sometimes we're willing to take bad consequences. Standing up to a bully might mean you get beaten up. But to you the act of standing up might be more important than not getting beaten up.

Director: So in this case you want to stand up and you do stand up, regardless of the bad part of the consequences?

Friend: Exactly. You're focused on the good part of the consequences — getting a reputation for courage, feeling proud, and so on. The good outweighs the bad.

Director: Then it seems we're saying something curious here.

Friend: What do you mean?

Director: We're saying that freedom is all about good consequences.

Friend: What's curious about that? Freedom is all about what you want. And what you want, in any act you perform, are the good consequences of the act.

Director: If freedom is being able to get the consequences you desire, you know what that means, don't you?

Friend: Yes. You have to be good at predicting the consequences of your actions.

Director: In other words, you have to calculate the consequences. So if we ask, what is freedom, we answer that freedom is calculation well used?

Friend: But that sounds crazy. Who would believe that freedom is calculation?

Director: You and I would, if what we're saying makes sense.

Friend: But you can calculate and fail to act on your calculations.

Director: Then you're not using your calculations well, right?

Friend: This just sounds wrong.

Director: Perhaps that's because we're overstating the case. Freedom isn't simply calculation. But calculation seems to be a part of freedom.

Friend: That's more reasonable to say.

Director: Now, what allows you to act on your calculations for getting what you want?

Friend: Courage?

Director: Is that because everything you want involves some danger?

Friend: No. You could want a piece of chocolate cake. There's no danger there.

Director: But if you had to steal the piece of cake?

Friend: Then there would be danger. But I don't like saying it's ever a matter of courage to steal.

Director: You're right to object. But if not everything involves danger, as in the case of having a piece of cake, what does this mean for what we're saying about acting on our calculations?

Friend: Sometimes you need courage, sometimes you don't.

Director: Do you think the same is true for calculation itself?

Friend: Sometimes we need it, sometimes we don't? I think that's true. Don't you?

Director: Well, let's explore it a bit more. When would you have no need for calculation?

Friend: When the consequences are obvious.

Director: You mean like if you are certain that if you eat too many pieces of cake your health will suffer?

Friend: Well, in that case you would have to calculate how much cake would be too much and not go over your limit.

Director: And that's a question of more or less, right? Then when it comes to obtaining something we want, whenever there is a question of more or less, we must calculate?

Friend: Yes.

Director: So if there's no question of more or less, and it's obvious to the point of certainty what the consequences will be, then we have no need of calculation as an aid in getting what we want?

Friend: Agreed. But I'm having a hard time thinking of any examples to support that claim.

Director: Do you think the claim is false if we're unable to think of any examples?

Friend: No, it would still seem true. But it would seem this is something to lay up for some time in the future, when a real life example might present itself. Then I'd know the claim is true. Then I'd know I can get what I want without even having to think.

51 DRIVEN

Director: What does it mean to be driven?

Friend: To be intensely attached to some goal or idea.

Director: Can an idea be a goal?

Friend: Sure. You might be motivated by the idea of being promoted, for instance.

Director: And this motivation is the key?

Friend: Yes, I'd say so. When people think of someone who is driven they think of someone who is highly motivated.

Director: But when people think of someone who is highly motivated do they think of someone who is free?

Friend: I think it's hard to say.

Director: Why?

Friend: Because there is more than one way to be driven.

Director: What are these ways?

Friend: The first is healthy drive, where you maintain critical perspective on the idea that drives you. The second is when you are a fanatic.

Director: And fanatics have no critical perspective on what drives them.

Friend: Right.

Director: Why do you think some people become fanatics?

Friend: Why? Because you don't have to think. You just have to believe that what you're doing is right.

Director: But a number of people seem to go through life without thinking, with simply believing that what they're doing is right. Are they all fanatics?

Friend: No, fanaticism takes something more. Intensity, as we've said.

Director: What accounts for a fanatic's intensity?

Friend: It comes of the single minded devotion to his idea. The people you're talking about don't have that, in all likelihood.

Director: Now, to be sure, we're saying that the fanatic is not free?

Friend: We are.

Director: And the one with healthy drive is in fact free?

Friend: Yes.

Director: He's free because of his critical perspective?

Friend: He is.

Director: Then I need to ask you, Friend. What is critical perspective?

Friend: It means being able to get distance on the idea that drives you.

Director: So you can see the big picture?

Friend: Exactly.

Director: Fanatics can't see the big picture?

Friend: No, they can't. They're too narrowly focused.

Director: But once the person with healthy drive takes in the big picture, doesn't he go back to his own narrow focus, his own idea?

Friend: He does, but then he periodically checks the big picture to make sure he is in a good way.

Director: What makes the way good?

Friend: His idea must be timely.

Director: What does it mean to be timely?

Friend: To be in accordance with the times, with the age in which we live.

Director: The idea must harmonize with the world as it exists today?

Friend: Yes.

Director: And if it doesn't harmonize it can't be a good idea?

Friend: That's how it goes.

Director: Can there be any healthy devotion to an idea that isn't any good?

Friend: No, there can't.

Director: So only the unhealthy will devote themselves to what we are calling untimely ideas?

Friend: Yes, I think that follows from what we're saying.

Director: This is a profoundly conservative way of looking at things, Friend.

Friend: How do you mean?

Director: I thought that ideas are things that can change the world. But what we're saying is that they're only any good if they harmonize with the world as it is.

Friend: Well, the world is a big place. The ideas in question can harmonize with a part of it.

Director: A part that wishes that things would change?

Friend: Sure, why not?

Director: Why not indeed. Now what of our old friend the fanatic? Does he want change?

Friend: Not necessarily. He might want to stop the world from changing.

Director: So he wouldn't be in harmony with the part of the world that wants change. But he would be in harmony with the part that doesn't want change?

Friend: I hate to say that the fanatic is in harmony with anything.

Director: Well, let's get back to what we said the difference is between the fanatic and the healthy one. Critical perspective. How does critical perspective affect the harmonies?

Friend: When you have critical perspective you can tell when you're falling out of tune.

Director: And fanatics are tone deaf?

Friend: Ha! I like that. Yes, they're tone deaf. They can tell that something is wrong, that the harmony is somehow bad, and they get upset. But they assume the problem is with everybody else. The healthy, on the other hand, admit when their own instruments need to be tuned. And they tune them.

52 INSTINCT

Director: Why do you think people often say to trust your instincts?

Friend: Because your instincts are generally more reliable than anything else.

Director: Yes, I gather that. But why do people have to tell others to trust something they know is reliable? I mean, shouldn't it be obvious to everyone that if instincts are as reliable as believed, then you would automatically follow your instincts? There would be no need to tell someone to do so. Do you see what I mean?

Friend: Yes, I do. Maybe it's because people forget.

Director: Forget something as important as the most reliable thing they know?

Friend: I don't know, Director. There has to be a reason.

Director: Let's come back to this. Now, what benefit comes from following your instincts?

Friend: What benefit? They say that when you follow instinct you do what's best for you.

Director: And what's best for you?

Friend: That varies from situation to situation.

Director: Indeed. But what's common from situation to situation?

Friend: I'm not following.

Director: If we say that each time we play a game there are different ways to play, does that change the fact that there's a common end we wish to achieve?

Friend: No, we want to win.

Director: Well, what's that common thing we aim at in doing what's best for us, regardless of how things might change?

Friend: Happiness.

Director: So it appears instinct is always instinct toward happiness?

Friend: Yes.

Director: Now where does freedom fit into this?

Friend: Freedom? Why do you ask?

Director: Because of a notion I have. You see, I think that there is an instinct for freedom. What do you think?

Friend: I think there is, too. Then instinct leads us toward both happiness and freedom?

Director: So it seems. How do those two, in your opinion, stand in relation to one another?

Friend: I'm not sure what you mean.

Director: I mean, is one a part of the other, or does one precede the other?

Friend: Freedom often precedes happiness.

Director: Happiness doesn't often precede freedom?

Friend: No, I don't think so — at least not as often. There are many people in the world who are sometimes happy but are never free.

Director: So if we have to choose, what shall we aim at, happiness or freedom?

Friend: Freedom, because you're more likely to be happy when you're free than when you're not.

Director: You're saying that we aim at freedom for the sake of happiness?

Friend: I am.

Director: Then why not just aim at happiness?

Friend: Director, if you want to build a house you need the materials first, right?

Director: Certainly.

Friend: Freedom is the material from which the house of happiness is built.

Director: You can't build a house of freedom from the material of happiness?

Friend: No, you can't. Happiness is the end, not the means.

Director: Very good then. We aim at freedom for the sake of happiness. Well now, do you remember that we said we'd come back to something? Do recall what this was?

Friend: Yes. We were wondering how people could forget to trust in instinct if instinct is the most reliable thing they know.

Director: Do you have any idea why people forget?

Friend: Maybe it's because it isn't easy to follow instinct.

Director: Let me see if I understand. You're suggesting that if something isn't easy, people won't do it, or do it very often. And if they don't follow instinct, or follow it very often, they'll eventually come to forget to follow it?

Friend: Yes. Not following instinct becomes a sort of habit.

Director: And it would be better if their habit were to follow their instincts?

Friend: I think nearly everyone would agree with that statement. Don't you?

Director: I do. But now here's something strange. Do very many people not follow instinct?

Friend: If not very many, then at least a considerable number.

Director: Do those who don't follow instinct sometimes prompt others to follow instinct?

Friend: I think they often do.

Director: Why do they?

Friend: Because you can think something is best despite the fact you don't live up to it, and you don't want others to make the same mistakes you made.

Director: Is not listening to instinct the biggest mistake you can make?

Friend: If what we've been saying is true, then yes.

Director: What of what we've been saying might not be true?

Friend: We've been assuming that we all have instincts toward freedom and happiness.

Director: You don't think we do?

Friend: I'm not sure. Don't you know people whose instincts just seem bad? No matter the situation, they're never happy or free. So listening to instinct might sometimes be a mistake.

Director: If that's true, then what should these poor people listen to?

Friend: I'm surprised you didn't offer the answer yourself. Reason, Director. Reason.

53 CONCLUSIONS

Director: Are we more free when we draw conclusions or when we don't?

Friend: I suppose it depends.

Director: On what?

Friend: The circumstances.

Director: Can you give an example of when concluding would make you more free?

Friend: Sure. Suppose you are in an abusive relationship. You conclude you should leave. You're on your way to being more free.

Director: And when would concluding make you less free?

Friend: If you conclude in the sense of passing judgment on people.

Director: How does that make you less free?

Friend: You're closing yourself off to the truth about the people you judge.

Director: But what if you're accurate in your assessment?

Friend: You mean what if your judgment is true? The problem is that when you judge you consider yourself to be superior to the people you judge.

Director: If you conclude that someone is untrustworthy, and you are right in your assessment of this person's character, you can't conclude that you, who are trustworthy, are superior?

Friend: We all have our flaws, Director.

Director: But some flaws are greater than others, no?

Friend: Don't judge unless you want to be judged yourself.

Director: But what if you do want to be judged? Isn't that conceivable?

Friend: Conceivable that you think the judgment will be favorable?

Director: Yes. Isn't that what every politician who runs for office does? He asks us to conclude as to his fitness, his character, his ability.

Friend: Politicians are conceited.

Director: All politicians?

Friend: Most.

Director: That's the conclusion you draw from what you know about politicians?

Friend: It is. And I think most people would agree.

Director: Well, let's get back to something you said. You said that passing judgment on people makes you less free because it closes you off to the truth. Do you still think that's how it is?

Friend: I do.

Director: Why?

Friend: Because you never have the whole story about someone. When you judge, when you draw a conclusion about someone, you are in effect saying I don't want to know any more. That's why we say don't jump to conclusions. There's always more information to be had.

Director: I suppose there is. But what if you don't jump to conclusions? What if you walk slowly and deliberately toward them? And when you arrive at one you hold on firmly. Don't you believe there can be a certain freedom that comes from that?

Friend: What freedom?

Director: The freedom of knowledge.

Friend: You're saying it's possible to know people, to really know them, without knowing everything about them?

Director: You can know people if you know the important things about them.

Friend: What are the important things?

Director: The things that go into what we call character.

Friend: What goes into character?

Director: The main ingredients? Beliefs and tastes.

Friend: What about actions?

Director: Actions typically follow from beliefs and tastes.

Friend: Beliefs makes sense. But what do you mean by tastes?

Director: What a person likes and dislikes, broadly speaking.

Friend: So if you think you know what someone thinks and likes, you conclude about his character?

Director: Yes. And that will make me more free because now I know something I didn't know, right?

Friend: But what if you're wrong?

Director: I stay open to that possibility and draw a new conclusion if I see I was mistaken.

Friend: So you're not really concluding.

Director: Of course I am.

Friend: When most people conclude they're done with the matter. They don't want to re-open the issue, even when they suspect they may have been wrong.

Director: That's likely because they don't believe that knowledge makes them free. If they did, and they valued freedom, they would do whatever it takes to be sure about knowing what they think they know, to be sure about drawing the right conclusions.

Friend: Knowledge about people is the most important knowledge?

Director: What could be more important?

Friend: And you can't have knowledge about people without drawing conclusions?

Director: That's right. But we should note that often times these conclusions are provisional conclusions. They need verifying.

Friend: And if you verify and find that you truly have knowledge about people, or certain people at least, how does this set you free?

Director: How does any knowledge set you free?

Friend: It only sets you free when you act on it.

Director: Then if you want to be free, you know what to do.

54 FEAR

Director: Can we be free if we're afraid?

Friend: Well, it depends.

Director: On what?

Friend: On what type of fear we're talking about.

Director: I didn't know there were different types of fear.

Friend: Of course there are. There's new fear and there's old fear.

Director: And with which of these can we be free?

Friend: New fear.

Director: What is new fear?

Friend: The fear we have when trying something new. It can be liberating to try something new. But it can also be scary.

Director: And old fear?

Friend: That's fear that lingers. Fear you live with. Fear that has become a part of you.

Director: Hmm. This makes me wonder.

Friend: Wonder? About what?

Director: About how complicated things might get.

Friend: Why would they get complicated?

Director: Well, what if you have a lingering fear, a fear very much part of you, one you live with — of trying anything new? Is that old fear or new fear?

Friend: I suppose you could say it's an old fear of new fears.

Director: Fear of fear?

Friend: I think that's possible, don't you?

Director: What about fear of the fear of fear?

Friend: Now you're being ridiculous.

Director: Am I? If you can fear fear, why not take it further?

Friend: Well, I suppose it's possible.

Director: I think this sort of thing may be what happens to those who suffer from chronic, debilitating fear. They probably don't even know what they fear anymore. They just know they're afraid.

Friend: There's no way people like that can be free.

Director: Agreed.

Friend: But how can they become free? Do they peel back the layers of their fear like you would an onion?

Director: However we describe it I think the point is the same. They have to identify the original fear.

Friend: And when they do?

Director: They must face it and overcome it.

Friend: What if they can't get rid of the fear?

Director: Overcoming doesn't always involve getting rid of the fear. But it does involve being very clear about what the fear is. You have to know your fear, and know it very well.

Friend: Like the saying 'know thyself'?

Director: Yes. You have to identify the fear in so many words, honest words to yourself. And once you have you have to manage your fear. You can't let it manage you.

Friend: What's your biggest fear, Director, the fear you have to live with, have to manage? Do you mind my asking?

Director: No, I don't mind your asking. My biggest fear is that I'm not living up to my calling.

Friend: Philosophy?

Director: Yes.

Friend: But, Director, you do live up to that calling.

Director: How many philosophers have you known?

Friend: Well, just you.

Director: Then how can you tell I'm living up to my calling?

Friend: You just... do!

Director: And how do you think I manage my fear?

Friend: Through constant philosophizing.

Director: But what if I'm not philosophizing in the right way?

Friend: But what's the right way?

Director: That's what I'm always trying to find out.

Friend: Well, I think you've already found it out.

Director: Thanks for the vote of confidence, Friend. But what's your biggest fear?

Friend: I'm afraid I'll never find my calling.

Director: Oh, but I thought you already had.

Friend: Why did you think that?

Director: Because of the interest you show in our discussions.

Friend: You think philosophy is my calling, too?

Director: Why not?

Friend: But I'm not as good at it as you are.

Director: I don't know about that. But even if you're not, do you think you have to be the best at something in order for it to be your calling?

Friend: Isn't that the idea of having a calling — being the best?

Director: No, Friend. Having a calling means to follow what calls you, regardless of how you compare to anyone else. The idea that you must be the best only leads to fear.

Friend: Fear that you won't be the best? So you're saying that's the fear I must overcome?

Director. Yes. And I don't think it will be easy. But I can tell you it will be worth the effort.

55 COMPLICATION

Director: Friend, do you believe you can be free if your life is complicated?

Friend: Complicated in what sense?

Director: Complicated like rope tied up in a great big knot.

Friend: Like a knot? No, I don't think you can be free.

Director: What do you need in order to become free?

Friend: You have to untie the knot.

Director: And if the knot won't untie?

Friend: Then you must cut the knot.

Director: What does it take to cut a knot?

Friend: Bold action.

Director: I see. That would seem to work well for external circumstances. But what if the knot is inside yourself? How do you cut it?

Friend: Oh, I didn't know we were talking about internal circumstances, too. You shouldn't cut internal knots.

Director: Why not?

Friend: You run the risk of damaging yourself.

Director: So you must simply, patiently untie the knot?

Friend: There is no other way.

Director: Now what about intermediary things?

Friend: Intermediary things? Like what?

Director: Works of art — a book, for instance. It's a product of the interior made external, no? What if an author writes something that's so complicated that no one can understand it? Is the book a sort of knot?

Friend: I think it is.

Director: And as with all knots, what's to be done?

Friend: Untie or cut.

Director: What's the difference between cutting and untying in the case of a book?

Friend: In untying you take the book on its own terms and try to work it through. It's sort of like being in a maze, trying to find your way out. But in cutting you bring external factors into consideration. You rise above the walls of the maze in order to see where the entrance and the exit are.

Director: The external factors let you rise above the walls? How?

Friend: Suppose you're reading a book on topic X, and it's a very complicated book, dealing with all sorts of other things, A, B, C, and so on. Well, suppose the author never mentions Z. But you know from your own life experience that there is never an X without a Z being nearby. And as you consider this you realize that Z is the answer to the riddle of the book. You rise above the walls.

Director: But are all complicated books like riddles, or only those that are designed as riddles?

Friend: It doesn't matter. Everything that's complicated is like a riddle waiting to be solved.

Director: Including internal complications, complications in one's thinking? You've said that you shouldn't cut internal knots. But can't you guess the riddle of the knot?

Friend: Well, I suppose riddle guessing isn't quite the same as cutting. So yes, let's say you can rise above the walls of the maze of the mind by means of a good guess.

Director: Now let's get back to external things. You said bold action cuts the knot in that case. Can you give an example?

Friend: Sure. You're tied up in an awful relationship with a member of the opposite sex. You simply end it.

Director: And that's the bold action that cuts the knot.

Friend: Exactly. But it may leave internal complications, emotional complications, that you'll have to deal with.

Director: Are emotional complications different than mental complications? I ask because I wonder if there are riddles to emotional knots, as well.

Friend: Emotional knots can be like any other knot.

Director: So we either work the knot through or guess the riddle?

Friend: Yes.

Director: But now I'm wondering, Friend. Isn't working the knot through, ultimately, the same as guessing the riddle? I mean, if you work the knot through, haven't you found the answer to the riddle?

Friend: I suppose you have.

Director: So if it's the same either way, why would you ever take the trouble to work something through if you can just guess correctly?

Friend: It isn't easy to make the correct guess.

Director: Would experience with other knots help you become a better guesser?

Friend: With similar knots, I suppose.

Director: Suppose you have a knot, and I have lots of experience with knots like the knot I see you have — can I supply you with the answer to the riddle?

Friend: You can, but I have to truly accept it and understand what it means.

Director: You have to take it in and make it your own?

Friend: Yes.

Director: And then you're free of the knot?

Friend: I'm free of the knot.

Director: But tell me this. Do you think there are those who would tie their knots back up again into a great big tangle after learning the answer to the riddle?

Friend: It's not a question of thinking that happens. I know it happens.

Director: Why do they do this?

Friend: They're so used to being complicated they just can't imagine being any other way.

56 JUSTICE

Friend: Can you be free without justice?

Director: What do you think justice is?

Friend: Getting what you deserve.

Director: And who decides what you deserve? You?

Friend: No, of course not.

Director: Why not?

Friend: Because if you decide what you deserve then where is the check and balance that prevents you from taking more than you deserve?

Director: Then who decides?

Friend: Well, no one really decides in the simple and final sense.

Director: If no one really decides, then that means that you never really know what you deserve?

Friend: You have an idea.

Director: Is that all that justice is, an idea?

Friend: Essentially, yes.

Director: Do different people have different ideas about what they and others deserve? Or does everyone have the same basic notion?

Friend: No, people have different ideas.

Director: So you might believe a criminal deserves punishment?

Friend: Of course.

Director: And you might believe a brave man deserves honor?

Friend: Certainly.

Director: But not everyone would share your beliefs?

Friend: That's right. Some people think criminals can't help themselves and don't deserve punishment. And some people despise the brave because they themselves are cowards.

Director: But you're sure that criminals deserve punishment and that brave men deserve honor?

Friend: I'm sure of it.

Director: And we're saying that there are those who are equally sure of the opposite?

Friend: Yes.

Director: Do you think it would be unjust for them to get their way, to have criminals rewarded and brave men dishonored?

Friend: Of course I do.

Director: Their justice is your injustice?

Friend: Exactly.

Director: How are we to resolve this dilemma?

Friend: I don't know. And that's why I came to you asking if we can be free without justice.

Director: I'm not sure I see the connection. What do you think freedom is?

Friend: Being able to live our lives as we see fit.

Director: What does this have to do with justice?

Friend: If the ones who believe the opposite of what we believe get their way, doesn't it interfere with our lives and our ability to live them freely?

Director: How?

Friend: If criminals are not only allowed to go free but are even rewarded, we'll have to deal with criminals in our daily lives — and the problem is magnified because the rewards will make these criminals insolent.

Director: And what about brave men being dishonored?

Friend: Could you stand to be dishonored?

Director: We can't live our lives as we see fit unless we're properly honored?

Friend: No, I'm not saying that. But being dishonored is different. It's an insult.

Director: And this insult would be so terrible that we wouldn't be able to live our lives as we see fit?

Friend: Yes.

Director: Well, no one likes to be dishonored, Friend. I, for one, think it would be better if true courage were honored.

Friend: I agree.

Director: So it seems you had the answer before you asked the question about whether we can be free without justice. You're saying that we do need justice, or at least not injustice. Right?

Friend: Right.

Director: But not any old justice will do?

Friend: Of course not. We need our kind of justice, justice according to our idea, justice as determined by our standards.

Director: So what do we do?

Friend: I think we surround ourselves with people who share our standards.

Director: And how will these people interact with those who live by different standards?

Friend: I think they'll interact with them as little as possible.

Director: But if they're forced to interact? What will happen?

Friend: I think there will be a sort of war.

Director: A war? One grounded in different conceptions of what's just? Who do you think will win?

Friend: If it's us against those who surround themselves with criminals and cowards? They don't stand a chance.

Director: Then why do you think we haven't already won?

Friend: Because we're only just beginning to fight.

57 ASSUMPTION

Director: Friend, do you believe that everyone is free?

Friend: No, I don't.

Director: Of those who aren't free, do you believe some of them assume that they are in fact free?

Friend: I do.

Director: Why do you think that is?

Friend: They're told they're free.

Director: So they must not know what freedom is.

Friend: That's the primary reason why they aren't free.

Director: If you know what freedom is, you're free?

Friend: No, but you can't be free without knowing what freedom is.

Director: If I tell you that you're a doctor, would you assume that you are in fact a doctor?

Friend: Of course not.

Director: Is that because you know what a doctor is and you know that you're not one?

Friend: Yes.

Director: But what if you don't know what a doctor is? Would you assume you must be one because I'm telling you that you are?

Friend: I wouldn't, no. But I believe there are some people who would.

Director: It's the same sort of thing as with freedom, no?

Friend: It is. You don't know what something is and when someone tells you that you are that something you simply assume it must be so.

Director: If I tell you that you're a doctor, and you don't know what a doctor is, wouldn't it make sense for you to try and learn what a doctor is?

Friend: Of course it would. And I would make an effort to find out what a doctor is.

Director: Then why don't certain people who aren't free, but are told they are, try to find out what freedom is?

Friend: Because it takes courage to learn what freedom is. It doesn't take any courage to learn what a doctor is.

Director: I agree. But doesn't this lead to something strange?

Friend: What?

Director: What if some of those who aren't free, but are told they are, go to the library and look up freedom?

Friend: I think that's a good idea. But what's strange about that?

Director: Do you think they can learn about freedom from a book?

Friend: I think they can. But it's only a start. They have to do more than that.

Director: Agreed. But if it takes courage to learn what freedom is, and they can learn something about freedom from a book — does that mean it takes courage to read that book?

Friend: Yes, I know what you mean. That does seem a little strange. But I think it's true. It does take courage to read that book.

Director: But courage aside, how likely is it that they will ever even go to the library?

Friend: Not very likely. They think they already know what freedom is.

Director: And we never look into something that we think we already know?

Friend: That's the way of it.

Director: So what can we do to help?

Friend: We can challenge them.

Director: What do you mean?

Friend: We can ask them questions about freedom.

Director: But can we do this if we ourselves don't know what freedom is?

Friend: Well, it would help if we knew. But it's not necessary.

Director: You mean if we don't know what a doctor is, and we ask someone who thinks he knows what a doctor is, what is a doctor, we'll be able to tell from his answer whether he truly knows what a doctor is?

Friend: Maybe not. Maybe we need to know what a doctor is first.

Director: So if we don't know what freedom is, we can't ask another questions about what freedom is?

Friend: Let's just say it would be better if we already knew.

Director: And if we already knew, why couldn't we just tell the person in question what it is?

Friend: Because that person assumes that he already knows.

Director: You mean he's not in the frame of mind needed for learning.

Friend: Precisely. He won't listen.

Director: So what do we do?

Friend: We ask him to tell us about freedom and point out places where what he assumes about it doesn't make sense.

Director: What happens then?

Friend: We let his pride go to work.

Director: What do you mean?

Friend: If he has any pride at all, he'll feel ashamed at not being able to give a good answer on such an important topic.

Director: And this will make him receptive to learning, being ashamed?

Friend: Yes. He wants to recover his pride. Learning about freedom can help him do that.

Director: What if he learns a thing or two and then assumes that he knows all there is to know?

Friend: We go back to raising questions with him.

Director: And if he gets irritated with us?

Friend: What's more important, *Director*? Keeping things smooth or helping someone learn?

58 Think, Obey

Director: Is it enough to think?

Friend: What do you mean?

Director: Is thought alone enough, or do you have to do something with your thought?

Friend: Well, you have to draw conclusions.

Director: And what do you do with your conclusions?

Friend: You act on them.

Director: And in acting on them, would you say you are obeying?

Friend: Obeying?

Director: Yes, obeying your thought and the conclusions that follow from them.

Friend: It sounds a little strange to say you obey your thought.

Director: What would you rather do with your thought?

Friend: Well, I... I suppose.... I don't know. But what if you're wrong?

Director: You mean what if you come to the wrong conclusions?

Friend: Yes. What if?

Director: Then you'll make mistakes.

Friend: But some mistakes can be very big.

Director: Oh, I agree. So it makes sense to think very carefully, doesn't it? But you know what the problem is, don't you?

Friend: No, what?

Director: If you're too careful, you're paralyzed.

Friend: Analysis paralysis.

Director: Yes. But that phrase can be misleading.

Friend: Why?

Director: Because if you're truly engaged in analysis you're the opposite of paralyzed.

Friend: Then when are you paralyzed?

Director: When you've stopped analyzing, or thinking, and are doing nothing but ruminating on what you've already thought.

Friend: How do you stop ruminating?

Director: By concluding, and then by sealing your conclusion with an act.

Friend: You obey.

Director: Yes. You obey yourself.

Friend: Do you think many people truly know how to obey themselves?

Director: Maybe not many, but certainly some.

Friend: And what of those who don't?

Director: They still obey.

Friend: I don't understand.

Director: They obey others.

Friend: Their thoughts and conclusions?

Director: Yes, but not always their thoughts. You can conclude without thinking, you know.

Friend: What are the conclusions based upon then?

Director: Whims, prejudices, emotions — anything but thought.

Friend: And even if they're based on thought, the thought may not have been good, right?

Director: Right. What do you think makes for good thought?

Friend: Correct premises and good logic.

Director: What is good logic a matter of?

Friend: Intellectual honesty.

Director: You mean being honest enough to draw the conclusions that must necessarily follow from you premises?

Friend: Yes.

Director: And in what do good premises consist?

Friend: Truth.

Director: So if the premise is, for instance, that money grows on trees, we know it's false?

Friend: Yes, of course.

Director: And it takes intellectual honesty to admit when premises are false?

Friend: It does. But that assumes you know, on some level, that the premises are false.

Director: Do you believe people have a duty to check their premises?

Friend: I do. I would even go so far as to say it is a sacred duty.

Director: Then I think we've revealed another sort of obedience.

Friend: Obeying the imperative to check your premises?

Director: Yes, but there's something important to note here. It's not enough to check some of your premises. You must check all of your premises, each and every one.

Friend: I'd take it further, Director. I'd say you also have a duty to check the premises of others — all of their premises.

Director: And what do you do if you discover that someone is operating under a false premise?

Friend: It depends on whether he is intellectually honest or not.

Director: If he is?

Friend: You do everything in your power to help him see the truth about that premise of his.

Director: And if he's not?

Friend: If he knows the premise is untrue, even if only in some foggy way, but holds to it anyway? There's nothing you can do. You just have to let him live with the consequences.

59 Oppression I

Director: When you're oppressed, how do you feel?

Friend: Over time? I think you become depressed.

Director: What's the cure?

Friend: Rebellion against the oppressor.

Director: Does rebellion only lift your spirit when it's successful?

Friend: No, I think the very act of rebelling has benefits for the spirit.

Director: Why do you think that is?

Friend: Because it's better to do something than to do nothing.

Director: Even if the oppression becomes worse after the rebellion?

Friend: Do you think that it's better not to rebel?

Director: No, I just think it's good to know what you're getting yourself into. Can you name a common form of oppression?

Friend: Sure. Political oppression.

Director: How do you rebel politically?

Friend: Well, you can protest, demonstrate.

Director: And if that's not enough?

Friend: If the oppression is bad enough? You turn to other means.

Director: Now what about in private life?

Friend: What do you mean?

Director: I mean, does oppression always have to be political?

Friend: Of course not. A simple bully can oppress you.

Director: And bullies come in all shapes and sizes?

Friend: Certainly.

Director: What's the most oppressive form of bully?

Friend: The one who has authority.

Director: You mean like a boss at work?

Friend: Yes.

Director: How do you rebel against a boss at work?

Friend: You resist.

Director: How do you resist?

Friend: You question what he tells you to do.

Director: Do oppressive bullies like to be questioned?

Friend: Certainly not. They hate it.

Director: Why do you think they hate it?

Friend: Because oppressors never act reasonably.

Director: Do you think that's true of all oppressors, or just the bullies in private life?

Friend: No, I think it's true of all oppressors.

Director: What's the opposite of an oppressor?

Friend: The opposite? One who lifts your spirits. One who inspires you.

Director: When someone is the opposite of another, does that someone use the opposite means?

Friend: I'm not sure what you mean.

Director: I just mean to ask if an oppressor is unreasonable, then must one who inspires be reasonable?

Friend: Oh, of course.

Director: And it's the reasonableness that inspires?

Friend: Yes.

Director: And reasonableness comes from the use of reason?

Friend: Right.

Director: Oppressors don't use reason?

Friend: No, they do violence to reason.

Director: Do you think they hate reason?

Friend: I do. And the ones who inspire love reason.

Director: Now, since we seem to agree that reason is good, I wonder if you'll agree to this.

Friend: To what?

Director: To the notion that if it's good to reason about some things, it follows that it's good to reason about all things.

Friend: I absolutely agree. And I think you've put your finger on what oppressors are best at, and how they stay in power. Oppressors do in fact reason. But they only reason about the things they want to reason about. They forbid reasoning about anything else.

Director: So they can claim to be reasonable, since they do in fact reason about some things?

Friend: Precisely. They know it's bad to have a reputation for being unreasonable. So they put on a show.

Director: And if you're in the audience, so to speak, during such a show, what's the greatest act of rebellion you can undertake?

Friend: The greatest act of rebellion? I would say that it's speaking up and reasoning about whatever the oppressor has forbidden you to reason about.

Director: And if you do this you can expect retaliation?

Friend: Yes, of course. But what does that matter? Rebellion lifts the spirit. And I believe it also lifts the spirit of many others who merely witness the rebellion.

Director: But that's the thing about retaliation, Friend — it's meant to crush the spirit.

Friend: But is that a reason not to rebel? Our spirits can only be crushed when we let them be crushed. And if our rebellion is great enough, won't our spirits soar?

60 CHANGE

Friend: Have you ever heard the saying the more things change the more they stay the same?

Director: I have.

Friend: Do you think it's true?

Director: Well, what do you think the saying means?

Friend: That everything always changes and that the only change possible is when things don't change.

Director: In other words, staying the same is a change from the status quo of change.

Friend: Yes. What do you think?

Director: Like most sayings, Friend, I think there's some truth to it.

Friend: Do you think it applies to people or just to their circumstances?

Director: I think it applies to both.

Friend: What does it mean if people are changing all the time?

Director: In order to know what it means I think we need to know what kind of change is possible for people.

Friend: I think there are two types of change — change in what they think and change in what they do.

Director: Then tell me, Friend. Is it possible to change your deeds without changing your thought?

Friend: It is.

Director: And is it possible to change your thought without changing your deeds?

Friend: Yes, certainly.

Director: When change happens, is that the way it usually happens, with one divorced from the other? Or is it more natural, or easier, to change both so that thought and deed are in harmony with one another?

Friend: I think it's much more likely both will change and keep in harmony.

Director: So if we see a change in what someone does it's likely his thought has changed?

Friend: It is.

Director: And if we discover a change in what someone thinks it's likely his deeds have changed?

Friend: That's right.

Director: But if one changes and not the other we have a sort of change in the world, yes? In other words, something remains the same.

Friend: Yes, that's true. But if one changes and not the other a stress is created, a stress that might be too much for the person to bear. It isn't healthy for thought and deed to clash.

Director: Suppose thought and deed are in healthy harmony. Why aren't we free to just go on doing and thinking the same things?

Friend: Because the world around us changes.

Director: And we must change with the world?

Friend: Do we have much choice?

Director: What happens if we don't?

Friend: We'll suffer from another sort of lack of harmony.

Director: Our not being in harmony with the world?

Friend: Exactly.

Director: What does the world demand, thoughts or deeds?

Friend: The world generally demands deeds.

Director: And that's because it can't always know the thoughts?

Friend: Right.

Director: That means that even though the world compels you to change what you do, it can't compel you to change what you think?

Friend: It can try to make you change what you think, but if it's true that it can't always know what you think, then it's possible to hold out.

Director: Meaning it's possible not to change what you think.

Friend: Yes, but we have the problem of harmony again. To change your deeds but not your thought creates tension.

Director: Enough tension to cause a breakdown?

Friend: Definitely, in some cases.

Director: So it's best either to change your thoughts along with your deeds, or never change your deeds in the first place?

Friend: I guess that's true.

Director: Now, we've been talking about two types of harmony — internal and external, the one of your thoughts and deeds, the other of you with the world. Which is more important?

Friend: They're both important.

Director: In the case of thoughts and deeds, we're saying that a lack of harmony might result in a breakdown. What happens if you're in harmony with yourself but aren't in harmony with the world?

Friend: Your life will be difficult.

Director: Difficult because you're not willing to change to suit the changing world?

Friend: For just that reason. And, incidentally, I think we now know what it means when people are changing all the time. They want their lives to be as easy as possible.

Director: But I'm not sure how easy their lives will be. Haven't you heard that change, true change, is very difficult?

Friend: But all that really means, in effect, is that it's very difficult to remain the same, right?

Director: That's clearly so, if the more things change the more they remain the same. But I think we've taken this saying as far as we should. Like many paradoxes it can shed some light. But if regarded as strictly true, it makes things dark.

61 SEDUCTION

Director: Do you think it's possible to be seduced into freedom?

Friend: I think it's more likely you'd be seduced into slavery.

Director: Why?

Friend: Being seduced usually implies something bad.

Director: How would someone go about seducing another into slavery?

Friend: He'd make false promises.

Director: Can you name one such promise?

Friend: Not off hand, no.

Director: Well, what's the opposite of false promises?

Friend: True promises.

Director: What do we call someone who makes true promises?

Friend: Honest. Honorable. As good as his word.

Director: And what do we call the opposite of seduction?

Friend: I don't know. Persuasión?

Director: How about disenchantment?

Friend: Yes, I think that's better. A seducer enchants you, puts a spell on you, and someone who disenchants does the opposite.

Director: Now, I think we need to say something about freedom. Is it a positive or a negative?

Friend: It's a positive, of course.

Director: What's the nature of this positive?

Friend: What do you mean? Freedom is simply good.

Director: And good is always positive?

Friend: How is it possible for it not to be?

Director: I suppose it might be possible if freedom is simply a negative — the absence of bad things, things like slavery and lies.

Friend: But then freedom would be a neutral, not a negative. Slavery and lies are negatives.

Director: Good point. So, if someone is disenchanted of all the negatives — the seductive lies that have led him into slavery and even the slavery itself, assuming it's nothing more than a spell to be broken — he's free?

Friend: He is.

Director: But if someone remains under the spell, won't things seem to be other than they are? Might slavery not seem to be a neutral state? Or worse, might slavery in a bad case even seem to be a positive?

Friend: Yes, I think it might.

Director: And what of freedom? Might freedom actually seem to be an evil to this person?

Friend: It very well might — and that would make him one sick individual.

Director: How often do you think this sort of thing happens?

Friend: More often than I care to think.

Director: How would we set out to cure these sick people?

Friend: I guess we'd just have to persuade them that freedom is good.

Director: But how can people know, really know, that freedom is good?

Friend: They get a taste of it and just know it's good.

Director: Are people inclined to take a taste of something they think is bad?

Friend: No.

Director: They would resist anyone who tries to have them taste it?

Friend: They certainly would.

Director: From their perspective, someone who tries to get them to taste freedom is a seducer?

Friend: Yes, I think that's true.

Director: But in reality the person is a disenchanter?

Friend: He is. He's trying to break the spell that has them believing that freedom is bad.

Director: Now, I'm almost embarrassed to ask, but do you think the disenchanter could resort to certain means?

Friend: What means?

Director: Means that would trick the sick people into tasting freedom.

Friend: But then the disenchanter wouldn't be as good as his word.

Director: That's true. But wouldn't he be better than his word?

Friend: It's a slippery thing you're suggesting, Director.

Director: Do you think there's a better cure for people who are sick as far as freedom goes?

Friend: Can't we just try to persuade them?

Director: When every word they hear us speak seems to them to be an effort to seduce?

Friend: I don't know. Maybe what you're suggesting is best.

Director: Maybe. But maybe not. I have my doubts about this method.

Friend: What doubts?

Director: I think they're much the same as yours. For instance, how can the people so tricked ever trust us again?

Friend: If they come to understand the reason for our tricking them, and to appreciate freedom, maybe they could come to trust us again.

Director: I don't know, Friend. Maybe it's really best to pass such people by. Freedom might not be for them, and it's as simple as that.

Friend: Let's try by honest means, Director. If they fail, so be it.

Director: Alright, my friend. So be it.

62 EXCESS

Director: What does it mean to take something to excess?

Friend: To go too far.

Director: Is it good to go too far?

Friend: Of course not.

Director: What happens when you go too far?

Friend: You pay a sort of penalty.

Director: You always pay a penalty?

Friend: I can't think of anything you can take too far that doesn't involve some sort of penalty.

Director: What if you take being healthy to excess?

Friend: But you can't take being healthy to excess.

Director: Is that because being healthy is a state and not an activity?

Friend: Yes. It's like being wise, another state. You can't be too wise.

Director: But in the pursuit of health you can train your body to excess?

Friend: True. If you over train you actually harm yourself.

Director: And that's the penalty.

Friend: It is.

Director: And in the case of being wise you can overdo it by doing... what?

Friend: You can try too hard to learn.

Director: You mean you so dedicate yourself to learning that you don't sleep, or eat, or exercise enough? You are totally focused on learning?

Friend: Exactly.

Director: And the penalty is that you make yourself sick, either mentally, or physically, or both?

Friend: Yes.

Director: And if you're sick you can no longer learn, or at least learn as well as you can when you're healthy?

Friend: I think that's true.

Director: So if there is a state you wish to achieve — wisdom, health — you can overdo the means, the activity, and you will pay the penalty as concerns the state?

Friend: Exactly.

Director: And the penalty can be either the diminishment or the complete loss of the state?

Friend: What do you mean?

Director: I mean, for instance, if you over train your body by only a minor amount, you simply won't be as healthy as you otherwise would have been if you hadn't trained in excess. Does that make sense?

Friend: It does, and I think you're right.

Director: But if you over train your body by a very great amount you might actually cause the complete loss of your health?

Friend: Yes, that might follow.

Director: And it's the same with wisdom?

Friend: It is. You can actually make yourself a fool by having a mania for being wise.

Director: So a great enough excess of the activity leads to the opposite of the intended state?

Friend: Yes, it does.

Director: Do you believe that's always the way?

Friend: Always.

Director: What about in the case of freedom?

Friend: What about it?

Director: Being free is a state?

Friend: Of course.

Director: What's the activity associated with this state?

Friend: I... don't know.

Director: But surely there's an activity. I mean, in the case of the state of health, training was the activity. And in the case of the state of wisdom, learning was the activity.

Friend: I believe you that there must be an activity associated with the state of freedom, but I just can't think what it is.

Director: But now I'm wondering, Friend.

Friend: About what?

Director: What if there is in fact no activity associated with freedom? Wouldn't that mean that there can be no excess associated with it?

Friend: You're suggesting that nothing we can do can diminish or destroy our freedom?

Director: That doesn't sound right, does it?

Friend: No, not at all.

Director: But then what's the thing which done in excess destroys freedom in the same way that health and wisdom can be destroyed?

Friend: Maybe it's not an excess, Director. Maybe it's a deficiency.

Director: A deficiency in what?

Friend: Thinking.

Director: Freedom demands thought?

Friend: I believe it does.

Director: And you don't believe there can be too much thought?

Friend: There's no danger of thinking too much. When you're tired of thinking you simply stop. You can't think any more. Now, sure, some people con-fuse other things for thought — dwelling on things, for instance. These other things can be taken too far. But thought itself can't. And so it's the perfect activity for the state of being free.

63 INTELLIGENCE

Director: Is freedom simply a status conferred on all citizens of a free country, or is freedom something you have to earn?

Friend: People have varying opinions on this subject, Director.

Director: Well, what do you think?

Friend: I think it's both. But I'm more concerned with the freedom that you have to earn.

Director: Now, when we earn anything, what do we need?

Friend: We need to work for the thing we wish to earn.

Director: So we work to earn our freedom, freedom in the sense which concerns you?

Friend: Yes.

Director: With any work, what guides it?

Friend: I'm not sure what you mean.

Director: Let me put it more generally. What guides anything we do?

Friend: Our intelligence.

Director: So our intelligence guides our work?

Friend: Yes, f course.

Director: Do you believe that there are those who do thoughtless things?

Friend: Certainly.

Director: And some people perform their work without thought?

Friend: Yes.

Director: Is working for freedom something you can do without thought?

Friend: No, and I would say that working for freedom, of all types of work, requires intelligence most.

Director: Is that because it's difficult to earn your freedom?

Friend: Yes, freedom is among the most difficult of things to earn.

Director: And it takes intelligence to overcome difficulties?

Friend: Well, maybe not all difficulties.

Director: What else besides intelligence can help you overcome certain difficulties?

Friend: Courage, determination — things like that.

Director: You think that courage and determination don't take intelligence?

Friend: Do they?

Director: What is intelligence, Friend?

Friend: The power of the mind.

Director: You don't think that bravery and steadfastness are reflections of power?

Friend: Of course they are.

Director: But you don't think they're functions of the power of the mind?

Friend: We usually think of these things as deriving from a strong heart.

Director: You mean a physical heart that beats strong and makes one brave, and so on?

Friend: No, not the physical heart.

Director: What then?

Friend: The part of the mind we call the heart.

Director: Which is not the part of the mind that makes us intelligent?

Friend: Correct.

Director: What part makes us intelligent?

Friend: The thinking part.

Director: You mean the part that thinks, oh, this scary man is trying to start a fight with me, so I'd better run away?

Friend: You make it sound ridiculous, but yes.

Director: But then couldn't this same part think, oh, this scary man is trying to start a fight with me, so I must stand my ground?

Friend: I suppose.

Director: And this is the intelligence doing this?

Friend: It is.

Director: And what follows from this decision of the intelligence?

Friend: Courage is employed.

Director: In other words, the intelligence directs the use of courage?

Friend: Yes.

Director: Now, if you are working to earn your freedom, there will be times when you must engage your courage?

Friend: Yes, to back up the decisions of the thinking part of the mind.

Director: And how does the mind know what decisions, what steps, should be taken toward earning its freedom?

Friend: It thinks the problem of freedom through.

Director: A problem as in a puzzle?

Friend: Sure, as in a puzzle.

Director: With a puzzle you know what the end state is supposed to be?

Friend: Yes, otherwise you could never solve it, except by accident.

Director: So before setting out to solve the puzzle of freedom, we must know what the end state should be?

Friend: I guess we must.

Director: Where will we discover this end state, the vision of which will guide us?

Friend: We'll see it in the hearts and minds of people we admire, people who're free. And if we're lucky, the next step to solving our own puzzle will become obvious when we do.

64 RULES

Director: Doesn't it seem that some people think freedom means having no rules?

Friend: It certainly does, Director.

Director: What happens to us if we have no rules?

Friend: Nothing good.

Director: So if we want good to come of our freedom, we need rules?

Friend: Yes, of course.

Director: Now, what kind of rules are we talking about?

Friend: What do you mean?

Director: Don't you know there are different types of rules? There are generally valid rules and there are universally valid rules. Generally valid rules hold for the most part, in most situations — but there are exceptions. Universally valid rules hold in all cases — and there are no exceptions. What kind of rule do you think is most conducive to freedom?

Friend: Well, the freedom to make an exception seems important to me.

Director: Do you think it's harder to make exceptions than never to make exceptions?

Friend: An exception is hard because you have to think through what makes it an exception, why it should be an exception. If you never make an exception you never have to think.

Director: Would you say never having to think is a sort of freedom?

Friend: I don't like to think of it that way, but yes, I think it is for some.

Director: Is there anything hard about never making an exception?

Friend: Well, never making an exception can create stress on you when the stand you take isn't popular, or there is other pressure on you to except.

Director: I see. Now, do you think that there are certain things that lend themselves to universal rules, while other things lend themselves to general rules?

Friend: That's my opinion. But I'm not sure how many people see it that way.

Director: You mean people are inclined one way or the other and tend to use the type of rule they prefer for all things?

Friend: Yes. You can say they prefer a certain type of freedom — the freedom not to have to make exceptions, or the freedom to make exceptions.

Director: Why choose the freedom not to have to make exceptions, aside from not having to think?

Friend: Certain people aren't comfortable unless they have the universal. The general scares them.

Director: Why does it scare them?

Friend: The general seems chaotic. The universal seems orderly.

Director: You mean it makes the world seem more safe?

Friend: Yes.

Director: Tell me, Friend. What sort of world do you want to live in?

Friend: You mean what sort of rules do I want to live by? I'd like my world to be mixed, universal and general.

Director: What's an example of a universal rule you'd follow?

Friend: Not to bear false witness. I would never break this rule. And I wish that everyone felt the same.

Director: And what about a rule you'd make exceptions to?

Friend: I can't really think of an example right now.

Director: Maybe you can't because rules tend to seem to be universal until the time comes for an exception, and that time isn't at hand?

Friend: Yes, I suppose you're right. But what do you think? Do you prefer a mixed world?

Director: I think we need to be able to make certain exceptions — but we should be able to think them through, as you said — to articulate why. And when we articulate why, we need to be on the lookout for rules that might follow from the exceptions we make. Exceptions can reveal new rules, and sometimes even universally valid rules.

Friend: So you feel the need for exceptions but are open to universals?

Director: I think that's fair to say. And isn't there advantage to proceeding this way? If we are articulating the reasons for our exceptions and looking for new rules as we go, won't the world seem, and in fact be, less chaotic?

Friend: Yes, it will have more reason and possibly more, and better defined, rules.

Director: Now, let's get back to the notion of freedom meaning no rules. Do you think it's truly possible to live with no rules, whether good comes of it or not?

Friend: I don't. And I think the people who talk about having no rules know it isn't possible, too.

Director: Then why do they talk about it if they know it's impossible?

Friend: They aren't the sort of people who care whether what they say is strictly true.

Director: And caring about the truth of what you say, is that a sort of rule?

Friend: It is.

Director: The ones who talk about the impossible being possible, why do you think they do, aside from not caring about the strict truth of what they say?

Friend: I can only imagine that they see it as something to strive toward.

Director: You mean having no rules is an ideal for them?

Friend: Yes, that's the most generous interpretation.

Director: So if they can pare things down to just a handful of rules, they're coming close to the ideal?

Friend: Yes, and I think they'd be very happy to have just a single rule to live by.

Director: What do you think such a rule might be?

Friend: I haven't got any idea. But I can tell you this. Anyone who lives by one rule, and one rule only, is a monomaniac.

Director: Yes, I suppose that's true. But now I wonder. Do you think they would hold that single rule as a general or as a universal rule?

Friend: A general rule, because an exception would leave them with nothing — their nirvana.

65 INHIBITION

Friend: Freedom means having no inhibitions.

Director: No inhibitions? Shouldn't you be inhibited to do something shameful?

Friend: Well, yes... but....

Director: And what about something bad or wrong?

Friend: You shouldn't feel free to do such things. But inhibition isn't about doing the shameful, bad, or wrong.

Director: Then when are you inhibited?

Friend: You're inhibited when you feel you can't do something good.

Director: You mean you think something is good but you feel it isn't?

Friend: Yes, exactly.

Director: So what you think and what you feel are at odds?

Friend: They are.

Director: Is there a way to bring them into harmony with one another?

Friend: I think you just have to bring yourself in line with what you think.

Director: You sacrifice feeling to thought?

Friend: It's not exactly a sacrifice.

Director: Is that because if you do what you think is good often enough, your feelings will eventually change, so that you'll feel good about doing the good thing?

Friend: Yes. It's called conditioning. You condition yourself toward the good.

Director: Well, that seems to make good sense. But now I wonder. How do you know something is good if it doesn't feel good?

Friend: You simply have to think it through.

Director: So you think to yourself that a thing must be good to do because.... Why?

Friend: Because you see the benefits that follow from the thing.

Director: The benefits that others experience?

Friend: Yes.

Director: Like feeling good?

Friend: Of course.

Director: But you have no way of actually knowing that doing the thing will feel good for you?

Friend: Well, no.

Director: You just believe you'll feel good, or come to feel good. You take a leap of faith.

Friend: I suppose that's true.

Director: And your faith is based on the fact that others say it feels good to them.

Friend: But it's more than just their saying it. You can tell they feel good.

Director: If you can tell, if you know, that something feels good to others, we're saying that you should trust their feelings over your own, the feelings which inhibit you?

Friend: Well, I'm not sure that's what we're saying.

Director: Aren't we? You see that something feels good to others, and would like it to feel good to you — but you don't do it because of negative feelings that you have about the thing in question. And what's the solution? To trust what others feel and do that something.

Friend: Somehow that doesn't seem right, Director.

Director: Then let's look at it a bit differently. If something doesn't seem good to you, and you have no desire to do the thing, would you be inhibited?

Friend: You wouldn't, no.

Director: You have to want to do the thing in order to be inhibited?

Friend: You have to want it, on some level. If you don't, then it's as simple as not wanting to do something.

Director: Now, there's nothing wrong with not wanting to do something, is there? But there's something wrong with being inhibited. I mean, it's not a good thing, right?

Friend: That's right.

Director: And the thing that's wrong is that there's a conflict, yes?

Friend: Yes.

Director: You want to do the thing, but you don't want to do the thing?

Friend: Exactly.

Director: So to rid yourself of inhibition you must resolve the conflict.

Friend: Yes. And that's where thinking comes in.

Director: Then do you think like this? I want to do the thing. I don't want to do the thing. One of these desires has to outweigh the other. So I must choose the one that does.

Friend: You're asking me if weighing desires is thought?

Director: Well?

Friend: Let's say it is — part of it, anyway.

Director: What do you do if the scales are equally balanced?

Friend: You have to tip the scales one way or the other.

Director: What if you tip the scales in favor of doing the thing, and you don't feel good when you do it?

Friend: Then it might be harder the next time to tip the scales to do the thing again.

Director: You mean you're hoping to condition yourself to feel good about what you do?

Friend: Yes.

Director: What if instead of feeling better about this thing over time, you merely feel the same, or worse? Could it be that you've tipped the scales the wrong way?

Friend: I guess that's possible. But then what does that say about what you thought to be good?

Director: It says you need to think again.

66 HAPPINESS

Director: Can you be free but unhappy?

Friend: Yes, I suppose that's possible.

Director: Can you be happy but un-free?

Friend: You're asking if freedom is a requirement for happiness?

Director: Is it?

Friend: Well, I think the un-free can have moments of happiness. But I don't think they can be simply happy.

Director: To be simply happy you must be simply free?

Friend: Yes.

Director: And if you are only partially free you can only be partially happy?

Friend: I think that's true.

Director: Hmm. Now I'm wondering.

Friend: What are you wondering?

Director: Maybe we were wrong to say you can be free but unhappy.

Friend: What should we have said?

Director: That unhappiness has the power to ruin your freedom.

Friend: I'm not sure I follow.

Director: Look at it this way. Do we feel — actually feel — free when we're unhappy?

Friend: I suppose you have a point. We don't. What do you think this means?

Director: I think it means we have to consider that there may be more than one type of freedom.

Friend: I'm listening.

Director: On the one hand, we have the freedom that makes happiness possible. On the other hand, we have the freedom that depends on happiness. Or doesn't this seem how it is?

Friend: No, that does seem how it is. I think you're right. Some freedom supports happiness. And some freedom is supported by happiness.

Director: Well, let's talk this through a bit. Where shall we begin?

Friend: Let's start with the freedom that is supported by happiness.

Director: Alright. How would you describe that freedom?

Friend: I think it has to do with freedom of the spirit. When you are happy you feel free.

Director: Is it possible to feel free without actually being free?

Friend: When you feel free you are free, at least in spirit. It's only if you use freedom in two different senses that it's possible to say that you feel free without being free.

Director: But are there in fact two different senses of freedom?

Friend: Yes, there's another sort of freedom.

Director: How do we describe this other sort of freedom?

Friend: It has to do with external things.

Director: What sort of external things?

Friend: It could be just about anything — legal freedom, financial freedom, and so on.

Director: I think at this point we'd do well to recall something we said.

Friend: What?

Director: We said the un-free can have moments of happiness, but can't be simply happy. To be simply happy, we said, you must be simply free. Do you remember?

Friend: I do.

Director: Is the sort of freedom that involves the law, or money, and so on — is that the sort of freedom you must simply have in order to be simply happy?

Friend: Yes, but it's only part of what you need in order to be perfectly happy.

Director: Is the other part freedom of the spirit, internal freedom? In other words, internal freedom, no less than external freedom, also supports happiness?

Friend: Yes, I think that's true.

Director: Now let's think for a moment about happiness. Is it like freedom?

Friend: In what sense?

Director: Is there an internal and an external happiness?

Friend: Why, no, there's only one, and it's internal, though it can express itself externally.

Director: So when we said happiness both supports and is supported by freedom, we meant only this one type of happiness.

Friend: Yes.

Director: Well, we said that external freedom supports happiness. And we said that internal freedom supports happiness. We also said that happiness supports internal freedom. Is there any doubt about what we've said?

Friend: No, it all seems true to me.

Director: So we're saying that freedom, all of freedom, supports happiness. But happiness only supports part of freedom, internal freedom. Does that sound right?

Friend: No, it doesn't.

Director: Why not?

Friend: Because it occurs to me that happiness can also support external freedom.

Director: How?

Friend: Would you agree that happiness can give you a certain strength, an inner strength?

Director: In at least some cases, yes.

Friend: In those cases, when you are strong in your happiness, wouldn't you be better able to strive for things, external things, difficult things that must be won for the sake of freedom? Your happiness would sustain you in your struggle.

Director: Interesting. But if that's true, then what do we conclude?

Friend: What else, but that freedom and happiness are perfectly paired?

67 CAREFREE

Director: Do you think it's good to be carefree?

Friend: Of course I do.

Director: What does it mean to be carefree?

Friend: To be without worries.

Director: What is worry?

Friend: Well, it's just... worry.

Director: Is it anxiety and the like?

Friend: Yes, exactly.

Director: And these things aren't good?

Friend: Of course they're not.

Director: So being carefree is a negative state.

Friend: What do you mean?

Director: It's the absence of worry and the like.

Friend: Yes, it's a negative state in that sense.

Director: Is there a positive state associated with being carefree?

Friend: I don't know what you mean.

Director: What about being careful? Do you think it's good to be careful?

Friend: Certainly.

Director: What does it mean to be careful?

Friend: It just means... to take care.

Director: When you take care, do you have worries?

Friend: Not necessarily, no.

Director: But you have things of which you take care, things you mind?

Friend: Of course.

Director: So you can mind your affairs without worrying about them?

Friend: Yes, I think you can.

Director: And if you're carefree, does that necessarily mean that you don't mind your affairs?

Friend: You're asking if you can be careful and carefree at the same time?

Director: Yes. What do you think?

Friend: I think it's possible.

Director: So carefree and careful need not be opposites, or rather need not be mutually exclusive opposites?

Friend: That's true.

Director: Now, what about being cautious?

Friend: You mean how does it relate to being carefree?

Director: Yes.

Friend: Well, if you are cautious to the point of worry, you can't be carefree. But if you are only cautious to the point of care, then being cautious is not opposed to being carefree, if what we've said about being careful is true.

Director: If it is, then we're sure that care, and caution, and all the rest are not necessarily opposed to being carefree?

Friend: Yes, we are.

Director: Because it's possible to be carefree, and careful, and cautious, and so on with any like state, all at once?

Friend: Yes.

Director: Now who would believe us, Friend?

Friend: What do you mean?

Director: I mean, won't certain people think our talk a bit crazy? We're telling them that being full of care and being free of care — the literal, obvious meanings of the words careful and carefree — need not contradict each other.

Friend: Yes, but they didn't talk it through the way we did.

Director: And do we expect they will all come to talk it through at some point?

Friend: I suppose not.

Director: So what of those who don't?

Friend: They'll go on thinking there is a contradiction where there doesn't have to be one.

Director: And if they see us carrying on as if there were no contradiction?

Friend: They'll think we're fools even though we're the ones who know the truth.

Director: Should we be afraid of truth just because others might not understand?

Friend: Of course not. We're not cowards.

Director: So we'll seem to deal in paradoxes when the truth is that we don't?

Friend: Yes. But are there many more seeming paradoxes?

Director: It sometimes seems to me that there are a great many.

Friend: Are they all of the nature of carefree and careful?

Director: Some are, Friend. But some seem much more difficult.

Friend: I'd like to learn about the difficult ones.

Director: We'll turn to them in good time. But what about your friends?

Friend: What about them?

Director: Should we try to talk the paradoxes through with them?

Friend: I think we should — with those of them who'll listen.

Director: You don't think some of them will?

Friend: No, I don't. Some of them will believe we're like children playing games with words. And they'll close their ears and minds. But the irony is that they're the children. They don't know what it means to think things through.

68 SLAVERY II

Director: What is slavery?

Friend: Being compelled to do something that brings you no gain.

Director: But aren't slaves given food, clothing, and shelter?

Friend: They are.

Director: And isn't that gain?

Friend: Those are necessities.

Director: But don't we all have to work for our necessities?

Friend: We get more than necessities from our work.

Director: So if slaves were given more than necessities for what they are compelled to do, they would no longer be slaves?

Friend: Well, they would still have no choice as to what they do.

Director: So the compulsion is the thing.

Friend: Yes.

Director: But then to the extent that we all are compelled to work for our necessities, we all are slaves?

Friend: Loosely speaking, I suppose, you can say that. But only loosely speaking.

Director: Because if we wanted to stop we could?

Friend: Not exactly.

Director: Then what's the difference?

Friend: There is honor in working freely, without compulsion from another man, for your necessities. There is no honor in being a slave.

Director: Who so honors us?

Friend: Why, all the others who are working for the same.

Director: Are we all equally as honorable, or are some more honorable than others?

Friend: Some are more honorable than others.

Director: And what is the criterion for this honor? Bringing in more gain than the others?

Friend: That's part of it.

Director: So the one who gains the most is more honorable and further removed from being a slave because of this honor?

Friend: Yes.

Director: Tell me. Do all slaves have masters?

Friend: They certainly do.

Director: And any gain the slave makes goes to the master?

Friend: That's right.

Director: What does the master prefer, a slave who brings him little gain or one who brings him lots of gain?

Friend: One who brings him lots of gain.

Director: He would want to encourage the slave who brings him lots of gain, so that he continues to bring him lots of gain?

Friend: Of course.

Director: When you honor someone, do you encourage him?

Friend: You do.

Director: Then wouldn't a master wish to honor his top producing slave?

Friend: I suppose.

Director: Now free people have bosses, correct?

Friend: Correct.

Director: Don't these bosses do the same as a master, praising the top producing workers?

Friend: But, Director, there is all the difference in the world between a slave and free man.

Director: What is that difference?

Friend: It's obvious!

Director: Then we should be able to spell it out in so many words quite easily, no? So what's the difference?

Friend: All I know is that a free man is free, and everyone but you knows what that means.

Director: Then tell me, Friend. What is freedom?

Friend: The lack of compulsion, compulsion from another and not simple, natural compulsion for the things we need.

Director: Bosses don't compel?

Friend: Of course they do. But you can quit and find another job. A slave can't quit. He would have to run away.

Director: And there are laws against runaway slaves?

Friend: Now you've put your finger on it. When there is slavery there are laws supporting it.

Director: So slavery is, at heart, a legal distinction.

Friend: That's right.

Director: And if our laws don't distinguish between slave and free, it's safe to assume we all are free?

Friend: Of course.

Director: But what of the subjects of a tyranny? Their laws don't refer to them as slaves. In fact, they sometimes refer to them as free. But can we really say they're free?

Friend: Well, in that case it's just a lie that the people aren't slaves.

Director: Could there ever be a lie that says someone is a slave when in fact he's free?

Friend: No. If the law says you're a slave, you're a slave. Always.

Director: But why is the law always truthful about slavery but not always about freedom?

Friend: Because law on its own can make you a slave, but law alone can't make you free.

69 Pride

Friend: Director, do you know they say that pride can make you free?

Director: I've heard people say that.

Friend: Do you think it's true?

Director: Well, let's talk it through.

Friend: Alright. Where shall we start?

Director: I would say an obvious question to start with is whether a slave with pride is in a sense free. What do you think?

Friend: I think that, in a sense, he's free.

Director: Then what comes next?

Friend: I suppose we should ask about a free man.

Director: Is a free man without pride in a sense a slave?

Friend: I think he is.

Director: So we seem to be saying that the distinction between slave and free hinges on pride.

Friend: We do seem to be saying that.

Director: But, of course, we don't mean this literally. I mean, are slaves freed simply because they have pride? Are people sold into slavery simply because they lack it?

Friend: Of course not.

Director: And yet we would seem to want to maintain that pride, in a sense, divides slave from free. Doesn't it seem important to know what this sense is?

Friend: Certainly.

Director: Can we know in what sense we mean if we don't know what pride is?

Friend: No, we can't.

Director: Then tell me, Friend. What is pride?

Friend: Pride is a feeling of self-worth.

Director: And that is all there is to distinguish between slave or free — a feeling?

Friend: I think it's more than a feeling. It's knowledge.

Director: So pride is knowledge of self-worth?

Friend: Yes.

Director: In other words, if you know your worth then you have pride.

Friend: Exactly.

Director: I think this sounds fine, Friend. But I have a doubt.

Friend: What doubt?

Director: What if....

Friend: What if what? Why are you reluctant?

Director: Because I fear I am about to say something that's disrespectful.

Friend: Disrespectful? What are you talking about?

Director: I fear I'm talking about something terrible, Friend.

Friend: Come now. It can't be that terrible.

Director: Will you promise if I say it that you won't hold it against me?

Friend: Say it, Director.

Director: I'll say it. But don't say I didn't warn you. What if you come to know your worth — but you're not worth very much?

Friend: Well you were right. That's terrible.

Director: But can you say why it's terrible?

Friend: It's terrible because you're asking, in effect, whether everyone is worth much.

Director: What's terrible about that?

Friend: What's terrible is that you're questioning the ideal of our age. We all are equal. We all are worth much.

Director: Worth much — or worth the same?

Friend: Both.

Director: But don't we know that isn't true?

Friend: How do you mean?

Director: Are the people who mean much to you the same as those who mean much to others?

Friend: Of course not.

Director: So the people who mean much to others might, in your eyes, be worth less to you?

Friend: But we know that in a sense, essentially, they have as much worth as anyone else.

Director: Can it be a matter of pride to be worth the same as anyone else?

Friend: It definitely can be in the sense of knowing you're as good as anyone else.

Director: Do you think that for certain people that's not enough?

Friend: Of course it's not. People also want to be different, special — not the same.

Director: Do they want to be better than others, worth more?

Friend: Yes, that's true for some people. There are always problem people. But most people want to be different, unique, while knowing they are basically the same.

Director: So we have two ideals — we all are the same, we all are unique?

Friend: Yes.

Director: And we take pride in both?

Friend: We do.

Director: And this double pride has the power to make us free?

Friend: This double pride is freedom itself.

Director: Then it seems we can safely bring our inquiry to a close.

70 FOLLOW

Director: What's the matter, Friend?

Friend: I've learned something about myself that I'm not too proud of.

Director: What?

Friend: I'm a follower.

Director: What do you follow?

Friend: What do I follow? No, the question is who. I follow you.

Director: Why do you follow me, if that's what you do?

Friend: Because I learn from you.

Director: Is learning bad?

Friend: Of course not.

Director: And following allows you to learn?

Friend: Yes.

Director: Then it seems that either following isn't bad or it isn't following that allows you to learn. Which do you think it is?

Friend: Following is bad. So if it isn't following that allows me to learn, what is it?

Director: You're asking me, basically, what you're doing when you spend time with me?

Friend: Yes.

Director: You are examining.

Friend: Examining you?

Director: No, examining the arguments.

Friend: But if I'm examining, I'm examining the arguments that you make.

Director: You couldn't be further from the truth.

Friend: I make the arguments? How do I do that?

Director: No, Friend. Neither one of us makes the arguments. We follow them

— together.

Friend: But even if we follow the arguments together, you direct where the arguments go.

Director: I can prompt us to go where the arguments lead. But the arguments themselves go where the arguments will go.

Friend: Do you really believe that?

Director: It's not a matter of belief. There's a certain necessity to it.

Friend: How so?

Director: Maybe it will become clear if we start following an argument about following.

Friend: Alright. How does the argument begin?

Director: Why don't you say?

Friend: Okay. The argument starts from the assumption that following is bad.

Director: Yes, I can see it does. Where does it go from there?

Friend: It asks us whether that assumption is true or false.

Director: What's next?

Friend: If the assumption is true, that following is bad, we know we need to avoid following.

Director: Where does the argument go now?

Friend: It asks us to consider that the assumption may be false.

Director: That it may be false that following is bad?

Friend: Yes. So if it's false, and following is good, we know we need to follow.

Director: Now earlier you asserted that following is bad. Does it still seem that's so?

Friend: Well, we can't simply draw that conclusion. We're engaged in following an argument now. Do we really want to say that the following pertaining to following an argument is bad?

Director: A good point. Where does the argument go next?

Friend: It shows us that there may be different types of following.

Director: What are those types? Is it clear?

Friend: There is following people and there is following an argument.

Director: Following people is bad and following an argument is good?

Friend: Yes, but I think the argument goes further.

Director: Why?

Friend: Because there are times when we must follow a leader.

Director: So we can't say it's always bad to do that, to follow people?

Friend: Right. And that means we need to say when it's good to follow people.

Director: Where does the argument go from here?

Friend: It wants us to see that it's good to follow duly appointed authorities.

Director: Like a general in an army?

Friend: Yes.

Director: Well, let's pause here and rest for a while. I wonder, Friend. Do you see what I see?

Friend: What do you see?

Director: I see that we traveled rather well along a path of discussion.

Friend: I do see that.

Director: Were you following me while I followed the argument just now?

Friend: No, I wasn't following you. I was following the argument, too.

Director: Does that make you the kind of follower you'd like to be?

Friend: I'm starting to think it does. But there's a lot more argument for us to follow.

Director: Yes, and about many other topics, too. But let's not forget that when we're done following we should go back and examine where we've been. That's where the real learning happens. But this is the way of it, Friend.

Friend: Then this is the way for me.

71 HOPE

Friend: I'm not sure it's always good to hope.

Director: When isn't it?

Friend: When you hope and hope for something mindlessly and never do a thing toward achieving what you're hoping for.

Director: I see. So you would distinguish between passive hope and active hope?

Friend: Yes, I like that distinction. Passive hope means you just sit around wishing for something to come true. Active hope means you strive to obtain that something.

Director: But what if it's a situation beyond your control?

Friend: Like what?

Director: Suppose you have a loved one who goes off to war. It's beyond your control whether that person comes home safely or falls in battle. And yet you hope he returns safely. Is that a passive hope, in the sense that there's nothing you can do?

Friend: Yes, I think it is.

Director: And do you think it's a bad hope?

Friend: No, of course not.

Director: So not all passive hopes are bad hopes?

Friend: True enough.

Director: Would you go so far as to say that some passive hopes are good hopes?

Friend: In the case of hoping for a loved one? Yes.

Director: Now, what about when it's a situation you can control, or at least influence?

Friend: Then passive hope is always bad hope.

Director: Because when you can do something about the situation, you ought to do something about the situation?

Friend: Yes.

Director: Can you give me an example?

Friend: Sure. You live in a colony under a tyrannical mother country. You hope to be independent. So you join with your fellow colonists and rebel.

Director: And you live on hope until the war is over?

Friend: You do.

Director: And do you think that's a bad hope?

Friend: Of course not.

Director: So not all active hope is bad.

Friend: I'd go so far as to say that all active hope is good!

Director: Even if you try to influence a situation that can't be influenced?

Friend: Some people would say that all situations can be influenced, however little.

Director: Do you think they're right?

Friend: We can always try, can't we?

Director: And if we try, and try, and try, and expend all the energy we might use for other things, and nothing changes, or even shows any sign that it might one day change?

Friend: Well, that would be foolish.

Director: Is it bad to hope foolishly?

Friend: It is.

Director: Then not all active hope is good?

Friend: True. But I think we're ignoring an important type of active hope that is good.

Director: What type?

Friend: The type that strives toward the ideal.

Director: What of it?

Friend: It's impossible to ever totally achieve the ideal. But you strive toward it anyway. And the closer you get the better off you are.

Director: Can you give me an example of a such an ideal?

Friend: Freedom.

Director: But can't we achieve that ideal?

Friend: Not totally. I mean, do you know anyone who is simply and perfectly free? Don't we all live under some degree of constraint?

Director: It seems you have a point.

Friend: So we hope to be free, actively hope, and take steps toward freedom.

Director: And we're not fools for constantly doing this, for endlessly striving?

Friend: We're the opposite of fools.

Director: Do you believe everyone can strive when it comes to this? Or is there ever a time when we might have a passive hope for freedom, a passive hope that's good?

Friend: Well, the only way we could is if we simply weren't able to do anything about obtaining freedom. I imagine this would have to be under a terribly repressive regime.

Director: So if someone in such a regime simply lights a candle in the passive hope of a freedom that's beyond his present ability to strive toward, you'd think that's alright?

Friend: I would, if we're right to assume that there's truly nothing else that he can do.

Director: Then tell me. Who's more likely to act toward freedom if and when opportunity to influence the situation ever does arise? The one who hopes passively or the one who has given up hope?

Friend: The one who hopes, certainly. Hope can be a spur to action. Hopelessness only leads to lethargy and despair.

Director: That's so even for those who are passive in their hope when they might be active? It's better for them to hope than to fall into lethargy and despair, if that's the alternative?

Friend: Yes. Their passive hope might one day prompt them to act.

Director: Then it seems we have our answer. It's always good to hope. The only exception is when our hope is foolish, when we hope against what proves to be the truly hopeless.

72 MONEY

Friend: Director, can I ask you a question?

Director: Sure.

Friend: Do you think you have to have money in order to be free?

Director: Well, if we say you can be free without money won't we seem to be flying in the face of common sense? I mean, without money you don't even have a roof over your head, let alone anything else.

Friend: But you could stay with family or friends.

Director: So you would, in effect, be making use of their money, the money that provides for the roof, and so on?

Friend: You would.

Director: Isn't that then, in a way, as much as to have money yourself? After all, what is money for except to be used? And if you have the use of another's property don't you, essentially, have their money at your disposal?

Friend: I suppose that's true.

Director: Then shall we say you can't be free if you have no money?

Friend: But if we do we run into trouble with our ideal.

Director: Our ideal?

Friend: The ideal that we are, all of us, free and equal. The ideal doesn't say we are all free and equal as long as we have money.

Director: So on the one hand we run into trouble with common sense, and on the other hand we run into trouble with the ideal? Which sort of trouble would you rather have?

Friend: Isn't there a third alternative?

Director: And what's that alternative?

Friend: You don't have freedom and yet you do have freedom.

Director: Please explain.

Friend: If you don't have any money you don't have freedom in the sense meant by common sense, but you still have freedom in the ideal sense.

Director: How clever. But now I wonder.

Friend: What?

Director: If someone had a choice, do you think he would take the exact opposite of your third alternative?

Friend: You mean he would rather have freedom in the common sense way than freedom according to the ideal?

Director: Yes. What do you think? Would he rather have the money?

Friend: I think he would rather have the fourth alternative.

Director: The fourth alternative?

Friend: To be both rich according to common sense and free according to the ideal.

Director: But if he had to choose?

Friend: If he simply had to choose? I'm afraid most people would take the money, Director.

Director: But why do you say you're afraid?

Friend: Because money without the ideal is bad.

Director: But can't you have both money and common sense?

Friend: Of course.

Director: Is common sense bad?

Friend: No.

Director: And yet common sense is without ideals?

Friend: Well, that's the way we've been talking about it, as if you simply have common sense on the one hand and the ideal on the other.

Director: But it's not that black and white, is it?

Friend: No, I don't think it is.

Director: In fact, isn't common sense filled with opinions that derive from our ideals?

Friend: I think it is.

Director: And what about the ideals themselves?

Friend: That's a little more difficult.

Director: Because if you fill ideals with common sense they're no longer ideal?

Friend: I'm not sure about that.

Director: Well, maybe common sense comes in when there are conflicting ideals.

Friend: How so?

Director: Couldn't it serve as a sort of referee?

Friend: Yes, you might be on to something there.

Director: And what about this? Do you believe it's possible to live up one hundred percent to the ideals we believe in? Or is it more a matter of striving toward them imperfectly?

Friend: Imperfectly, no doubt.

Director: What fills the gap between the perfect and the imperfect, but common sense?

Friend: Nothing.

Director: So when we strive for the ideal of freedom, perfect freedom, we rely, where we fall short, upon the common sense notion of freedom, that which involves money?

Friend: I think that's true. But what if people don't strive for the ideal, any ideal?

Director: You mean not at all? Not even insofar as the ideal is embedded in common sense?

Friend: Yes.

Director: Don't you know, Friend? They will, in the end, likely become slaves to their money. Or don't you think that's how it is?

Friend: No, I do think that's how it is. I've noticed that, absent any other ideal, money almost always fills the void and becomes itself a sort of perverted ideal, a tyrant of an ideal. It's no longer money for the sake of freedom. It's money for the sake of money. And when that which is simply means becomes the end, you've lost your way.

73 MUSIC

Director: Friend, do you believe that music can give you a sense of freedom?

Friend: Believe? I know it can.

Director: Is this sense of freedom somehow simulated or is it the real thing?

Friend: Feeling free is feeling free, Director.

Director: And feeling free can come from different types of feeling?

Friend: What do you mean?

Director: I mean, can't music make you feel joy?

Friend: Of course it can.

Director: And joy makes you feel free?

Friend: Certainly.

Director: And what about sorrow? Can music make you feel that?

Friend: It can.

Director: And do you feel free when you feel sorrow?

Friend: You do when music makes you feel it.

Director: But not when you feel it, for lack of a better phrase, for real?

Friend: True. No one feels free when he feels real sorrow.

Director: Then why do you feel free when music makes you feel sorrow?

Friend: It's cathartic.

Director: What does that mean?

Friend: It's a spiritual release.

Director: I see. Now tell me. Is there really no difference between the joys and sorrows that come from music as opposed to those that come from real life?

Friend: The joys and sorrows of music are fleeting.

Director: Is that the only difference?

Friend: What you feel is what you feel in either case. But real life tends to give you joys and sorrows that last.

Director: But the sorrow that doesn't last, the sorrow of music, is good. Does that mean that a sorrow in real life that doesn't last is good?

Friend: It's better than one that lasts. But I know what you mean. No, it isn't good.

Director: It's only good when we know it isn't real? Isn't that how it is when sorrow is depicted by means of any type of art?

Friend: Yes, I think that's so. Sad movies, for instance, which we know aren't real, can bring us release. But I think music is the most pure when it comes to this.

Director: Why?

Friend: Because music touches the soul more directly than any other art.

Director: Does it touch the soul of the musician?

Friend: Well, that depends.

Director: You mean the musician might not actually feel the sorrow he makes others feel?

Friend: Right.

Director: But which do you prefer, the musician who feels the sorrow or one who doesn't?

Friend: I prefer one who does.

Director: And do you prefer the one who feels the sorrow in the same way that the audience feels it, or the one who feels it for real, feels it from his own life?

Friend: The one who feels it from his own life, the one who is sincere.

Director: In that case he would make the audience feel free while not feeling free himself? After all, we've said that no one feels free when he feels real sorrow.

Friend: But it's different for a musician or any other performer.

Director: How?

Friend: There's a release, a certain freedom, that comes from singing your sorrow.

Director: You mean it's good for the singer?

Friend: Yes.

Director: So the sincere singer of a sad song would be worse off if he didn't sing his song?

Friend: Don't you think it's true?

Director: There may be some truth in what you say. Or maybe you're just trying to make us feel better about enjoying the suffering of another.

Friend: But he enjoys the performance!

Director: So we're not enjoying his suffering, we're enjoying his enjoyment?

Friend: Exactly, his enjoyment brought into high relief by his suffering.

Director: Well, who am I to say about these things? But I have a question. Does everyone enjoy sorrowful and joyful music equally, or do people sometimes prefer one or the other type?

Friend: People often prefer one or the other.

Director: What does it mean to prefer sorrowful music?

Friend: I think it means there is a sadness in your soul, a sadness that the music touches.

Director: A sadness that not even the joy of music can penetrate?

Friend: For some people I think that's true.

Director: And what of those who prefer joyful music? Do they have a joy in their souls, a joy that the music touches? A joy that the sorrow of music can't penetrate?

Friend: I suppose that's so for certain people.

Director: Now if you could choose, which would you be? One with sorrow in your soul or joy?

Friend: You think I'll say joy. But what if I don't? What if I like the sweet sorrow in my soul and the sad music that gives it release, that makes me feel free? Does that make me bad?

Director: No, not bad, my friend. But worthy of pity.

74 CHOICE

Friend: Would you agree that freedom means being able to choose?

Director: You mean that freedom is simply choice?

Friend: Don't you think it is?

Director: But what if you can only choose between two bad alternatives? Is that freedom?

Friend: No, I suppose it isn't.

Director: Then is freedom having at least one good alternative?

Friend: Yes.

Director: But then is it really much of a choice? I mean, who would choose the bad alternatives over the good alternative?

Friend: Well, no one would.

Director: So freedom means being able to choose between at least two good alternatives?

Friend: I guess.

Director: But why did you ask?

Friend: Oh, I asked because I wanted to tell you about something I'm writing for my philosophy class.

Director: What is it?

Friend: We were asked to come up with a hard question.

Director: And what is your question?

Friend: It assumes that freedom is being able to choose. But it also assumes that in order to be free we need to make informed choices.

Director: You mean we basically have to know whether the alternatives are good or bad?

Friend: Yes, exactly. So here's the question. If you're not informed, would you let someone who is choose for you?

Director: You're asking if you would surrender your freedom to one of superior knowledge?

Friend: I didn't think about it in those terms, but yes.

Director: Well, Friend, here's a problem I see with your question. Can't the informed person inform you and allow you to choose for yourself?

Friend: That's a good point. I hadn't thought of that. But I see a problem.

Director: What?

Friend: How would you know you're really being informed and not misled?

Director: I guess you wouldn't always know. So perhaps you need to get a second opinion.

Friend: You mean like we do with doctors?

Director: Yes.

Friend: What if we get a second opinion, and a third opinion, and so on — and they are all the same?

Director: If you get three or more opinions and they're all the same, it seems likely you're being properly informed.

Friend: So does that leave you with any choice?

Director: Are we still of the opinion that we need at least two good alternatives in order to be free?

Friend: Yes.

Director: And shall we suppose the opinion of the doctors is that you need surgery?

Friend: Let's.

Director: And the only alternatives you have are surgery or no surgery?

Friend: Those are the only two

Director: Are those both good alternatives?

Friend: I'm more inclined to say they are both bad alternatives.

Director: So you have no freedom in this situation, if what we were saying before is true?

Friend: That's how it seems.

Director: But does that really make much sense?

Friend: What do you mean?

Director: I mean you really are free to choose. You can choose to have surgery. You can choose not to have surgery. Would anyone in his right mind deny that you have free choice?

Friend: You mean it's just common sense?

Director: Yes. Or do you think philosophy should ignore common sense?

Friend: No, I don't.

Director: Then let's get back to the question of being informed.

Friend: Alright.

Director: Suppose you only consult one doctor, and let's suppose you don't know him and have no way of knowing whether he is competent or not. He tells you that you need surgery. Are you well informed?

Friend: No.

Director: Why not?

Friend: Because you're merely taking what he says on faith.

Director: Would that change if you saw a diploma from an elite medical school with his name on it on his office wall?

Friend: That might make you better informed about him. But he might practice radical medicine, and you wouldn't know that unless you got other opinions or did some kind of independent research.

Director: But let's say you don't. Let's say you take him on faith. Is your choice between surgery and no surgery any less of a choice?

Friend: No. It's possible to make uninformed choices. That's just common sense, right?

Director: Right. But are uninformed choices free choices?

Friend: They're not. How can you be said to freely choose if you don't even know what you're choosing? That's just common sense.

Director: Yes. Now let's try and think up a better question for your class.

75 BEFORE

Friend: Do you believe there has always been freedom in the world?

Director: You mean was there a time before freedom?

Friend: Yes.

Director: It's hard to say.

Friend: Well, I believe there wasn't always freedom.

Director: Then how did freedom come about?

Friend: Imagine freedom is fire, a flame.

Director: Alright.

Friend: How do you think man first discovered fire?

Director: I don't know. How do you think he did?

Friend: Accidentally. A lightning bolt struck a tree and set it ablaze. Something like that.

Director: And once this accident happened man had to learn to make fire himself, or did he simply never let that first blaze go out?

Friend: No, he learned how to make fire.

Director: When man makes fire, would you say that the fire is artificial?

Friend: I don't know that I'd ever call fire artificial. Fire is simply fire.

Director: And is it the same with freedom?

Friend: Yes. Freedom is simply freedom, however it comes about, accidentally or deliberately made by man.

Director: Now, once man has learned to make fire, what must he do?

Friend: I'm not sure what you mean.

Director: Mustn't he secure a supply of wood or other fuel to burn?

Friend: Yes, he must.

Director: Then what about our metaphor? If fire is freedom, the fuel is... what?

Friend: I don't know.

Director: But this is very important, don't you think?

Friend: I do.

Director: What's your best guess?

Friend: Do you want me to say whatever comes to mind?

Director: Why not?

Friend: Bad ideas.

Director: Bad ideas?

Friend: What can I say? That's what came to mind.

Director: Now really, Friend, you surprise me. Why bad ideas?

Friend: Why not? Aren't bad ideas worthy of being burned up?

Director: Can you give me an example of a bad idea?

Friend: Sure. Slavery. Not only is it bad for the slave, it's bad for the soul of the master, and it's bad for the overall economy. So it's a bad idea all around.

Director: Then we throw the idea of slavery onto the fire of freedom and we are free?

Friend: Don't you agree?

Director: I agree that slavery is an idea that burns very well. But now I wonder. Do we really want to say that the flame of freedom depends on slavery and whatever other bad ideas there are in the world?

Friend: You're worried that something good depends on something bad? Why shouldn't it? There's no shortage of bad ideas in the world, so there's no danger we'll run out of fuel any time soon. Or would you rather we say that good ideas are the fuel?

Director: I'd rather we examine our fire metaphor from a somewhat different perspective.

Friend: What perspective?

Director: Let's question one of our assumptions and see how things look. What if there has always been freedom?

Friend: Always, meaning eternally, for all time?

Director: Yes. Would our metaphor have to change?

Friend: Well, we could still say that freedom is a flame. It would just be one that has always burned and will always burn, forever.

Director: And what about the fuel? Don't we need a supply of it that has always existed and will always exist, forever?

Friend: We do. And that's why bad ideas are perfect.

Director: Because try as we might to get rid of them, we can't?

Friend: That's right.

Director: Do you think there was a first bad idea, one that preceded all the others? Or have all the bad ideas there are always existed?

Friend: I think there was a first bad idea.

Director: Can you say what it was?

Friend: Well, you see, the first bad idea, as I see it, was to say yes when no was required, or no when yes was required. Does that make sense? I don't know what to call this idea.

Director: Maybe we should just call it the idea of the false. But was this idea always on fire with the flame of freedom, or did something have to ignite the blaze?

Friend: Something ignited the blaze, but it happened before the beginning of time.

Director: Alright. Then how did freedom come about? How was the fire lit?

Friend: There was an original good idea, the idea of the true, and when this idea struggled with the idea of the false sparks flew, the bad idea caught fire, and freedom was born. How's that?

Director: Not too bad.

Friend: Do you think others would benefit from hearing this account?

Director: I do, if only to prompt them to offer up a better one themselves.

76 Oppression II

Friend: Director, in the past, when we've talked about freedom, we've often talked about its opposite. Do you remember?

Director: Yes.

Friend: Do you remember what we said that opposite is?

Director: Why don't you tell me?

Friend: Alright, I will. We said the opposite of freedom is slavery.

Director: Do you think that isn't true?

Friend: No, I think it's true. But I think we're ignoring something else, something important.

Director: Another opposite?

Friend: Yes, but I think it encompasses slavery.

Director: Encompasses slavery? What is it, Friend?

Friend: Oppression. Don't you agree that slavery falls under the heading of oppression?

Director: Yes, and we'd be hard pressed to find anyone who'd disagree.

Friend: Well, I think we need to talk about oppression.

Director: What shall we say?

Friend: What we always say. What oppression is, what we can do about it. You know.

Director: And you expect I can hold up my end of the conversation just like that, on demand?

Friend: I know you can.

Director: But what if I say a demand for conversation seems oppressive to me now?

Friend: You're asking if I would oppress you?

Director: Yes, Friend.

Friend: Well, that's a problem.

Director: Why is it a problem?

Friend: Because I had a definition of oppression that I wanted to share with you that I thought was pretty good.

Director: But now you don't think it's good? Why?

Friend: Because you're suggesting that being made to do something you don't want to do is oppression. My definition says the opposite.

Director: It says oppression is when you're prevented from doing something you should be free to do?

Friend: Yes.

Director: But there's nothing wrong with your definition, Friend. We just need to add to it to make it complete. So we'll say that oppression is when you're prevented from doing something you should be free to do, or made to do something you should be free not to do. What do you think?

Friend: I think it's great.

Director: Well, now that I'm warming up to our talk, there's something I wonder about.

Friend: What?

Director: Assuming we know what oppression is, and our good definition gives me some confidence we do, don't we need to know something else, something equally important?

Friend: What do you have in mind?

Director: Is the object of oppression always the same, or do different oppressors focus on different types of things?

Friend: They focus on different types of things.

Director: And what are the basic types of things they focus on?

Friend: The basic types? I'm not sure. What do you think they are?

Director: Well, it seems there are three — the things you do, the things you say, and the things you think. Against which of these do you think oppression is worst?

Friend: Against deeds and speech.

Director: Why?

Friend: Because you can't know what people think. So you can't control what they think.

Director: But if you could know what people think?

Friend: Then oppression against thought would be worst.

Director: Then it seems it's worst — because we can pretty much know what others think.

Friend: How?

Director: By what they do and what they say.

Friend: But you can think it's bad to do something and then say good things about it and do it anyway. When that happens, can we really tell what you think?

Director: You have a point. But then we have to ask — what good is thought if you can't speak about it or act on it?

Friend: It's better than nothing.

Director: But wouldn't it cause tension to think one thing and say and do something else?

Friend: It would.

Director: And if this tension never finds release in speech or deed?

Friend: Then there's a problem.

Director: Might someone with no release conclude that it's better not to think, or at least not to think things that he's not supposed to think? In other words, might he not give up?

Friend: Yes. And then the oppressor wins.

Director: What's the only way the oppressor doesn't win?

Friend: If we can find ways to release our thoughts.

Director: Would such release make us enemies of the oppressor?

Friend: No doubt.

Director: Then may we always have the courage to find our release.

77 Discipline

Director: What is it, Friend?

Friend: I'm trying to figure something out.

Director: What?

Friend: I'm embarrassed to say.

Director: Why?

Friend: Because it's something I read in a fortune cookie.

Director: Those cookies at times give sage advice.

Friend: Don't they? Well, maybe I'll tell you. The cookie said that you must limit your freedom in order to maximize your freedom.

Director: Ah, a paradox. Not unusual for cookies to utter.

Friend: What do you think it means?

Director: I suspect it's about discipline, Friend.

Friend: Discipline?

Director: Haven't you heard that discipline can give you freedom?

Friend: Yes. But does discipline really limit your freedom?

Director: When you're free, are you free to do whatever you feel like doing?

Friend: Well, not exactly.

Director: Why aren't you free to do whatever you feel like doing?

Friend: Because sometimes you feel like doing bad things.

Director: What sort of bad things?

Friend: Let's say there are certain people you'd like to punch in the face.

Director: Why don't you?

Friend: Because you don't want to go to jail.

Director: So you want to do something but you know that that something will have bad results?

Friend: Yes.

Director: And it takes discipline not to do that thing?

Friend: I suppose it does, when you're provoked. But that's not really a case of limiting your freedom. You're not free to punch someone. It's against the law.

Director: Well, what's something that takes discipline that isn't against the law?

Friend: It could be anything, anything you think would be bad to do but want to do. That's when you need discipline.

Director: You mean, for instance, you want to eat fortune cookies all day every day, which would be bad to do, and you need discipline not to?

Friend: Yes. You're free to eat the cookies. But if you do, excessively, your health will suffer, and that would lessen your freedom.

Director: So you exercise discipline to limit the freedom with which you eat the cookies for the sake of a greater freedom, the freedom that comes with health?

Friend: Exactly.

Director: Then it seems your fortune cookie spoke truth. But shall we explore a bit further?

Friend: Sure.

Director: What is it in you that applies the discipline?

Friend: The will.

Director: And what does it discipline?

Friend: What do you mean?

Director: I mean, does your will tell your will not to will things it doesn't want to will?

Friend: No.

Director: Then what does will discipline?

Friend: I suppose it must be the desires.

Director: And it disciplines by commanding?

Friend: Yes.

Director: Regardless if the desires want to listen or not?

Friend: The desires never want to listen.

Director: What kind of rule is it over unwilling subjects?

Friend: Tyrannical?

Director: So will is a tyrant?

Friend: I'm not so sure, Director.

Director: Is that because we know that will power is good, while the power of tyrants is bad?

Friend: Precisely.

Director: Well, let's look at it like this. Are tyrants the rightful rulers of their subjects?

Friend: Of course they're not. No tyrant is a rightful ruler.

Director: Is will the rightful ruler of the desires?

Friend: If will isn't, I don't know what else could be. So will must be the rightful ruler.

Director: Then that would mean that will can't be a tyrant, unless....

Friend: Unless?

Director: What would happen if will attempted to rule a part of the soul, or being, of which it isn't the rightful ruler?

Friend: Will might become a tyrant. But what part are you thinking of?

Director: The mind. In fact, isn't the mind the rightful ruler of the will? Doesn't it tell the will what's good and what's no good when it comes to the desires?

Friend: Yes, I think that's true.

Director: Then mind rules will as will rules desire. And this is the discipline that keeps us free.

78 DEBATE

Director: What are you doing, Friend?

Friend: I'm preparing for the debate.

Director: Oh, well I won't bother you then.

Friend: You're not bothering me.

Director: But you're in the middle of something important.

Friend: I don't believe you really think that.

Director: You don't think that I think debates are important?

Friend: What's so important about them?

Director: Now, when someone who is earnestly preparing for a debate asks you why debates are important, what are you to think?

Friend: You want to know why I'm asking you? If you give me a good reason why debates are important maybe that will inspire me to prepare properly.

Director: Well, how can I refuse? You want to know what's important about debate? It's simple enough to tell you. Debate is a key ingredient in the recipe for freedom.

Friend: But you're talking about free and open debate between people?

Director: Of course. Why, what did you think I might be talking about?

Friend: I thought you were going to turn things around and talk about internal debate.

Director: Internal dialogue you mean?

Friend: Yes. Debate, dialogue — whatever you want to call it.

Director: But isn't there all the difference in the world between debate and dialogue?

Friend: What's the difference?

Director: Really, Friend. Now I'm glad I happened upon you. Don't you know that the object of a debate is to win?

Friend: The object for each of the sides, yes. But the object of the debate as a whole? Isn't it to arrive at the truth? And in that sense, isn't it no different than dialogue?

Director: But it is different. In a debate, one side generally has some of the truth while the other side has more of it, right? But at the end of the debate, both sides still have only the same amount of truth they started out with. But at the end of a dialogue, if all goes well, both participants will have more of the truth than they started out with.

Friend: But what's to stop a debater from making the arguments he must make for his side to win while being persuaded, while gaining truth, secretly, by and from the other side?

Director: Nothing, I suppose. But if you're persuaded that there is truth with the other side, why would you go on arguing against it?

Friend: Why wouldn't you? Debate is a sort of game. Arguing against the other side's truth is part of it. Do you see anything wrong with playing as long as you know it's just a game?

Director: Do I see anything wrong with playing with the truth? Is that what you're asking me, Friend?

Friend: So what do you suggest I do if I tell you, as I'm telling you right now, that the other side has the better case?

Director: You should go over to the other side.

Friend: Ha! You think it's that simple?

Director: Why not? Isn't debate a sort of game? See if you can get yourself traded to the other team.

Friend: But what if I told you that the only reason I would do that is so I can win?

Director: Then I would say you're motivated more by victory than truth. But then you wouldn't be any different than most debaters as far as that goes.

Friend: And those who engage in dialogue are all motivated by truth?

Director: No, certainly not. There are a number of people who are simply motivated by a love of winning arguments, when they should be motivated by the spirit of dialogue.

Friend: What's the spirit of dialogue?

Director: Partnership. Approaching the truth together. Helping each other see.

Friend: That's very different than the spirit of debate. But what about internal dialogue?

Director: What about it?

Friend: How can you have partnership, and so on, with yourself?

Director: Have you ever heard the phrase being at odds with yourself?

Friend: Of course.

Director: What do you think that means?

Friend: Well, it suggests that we are made up of different parts that aren't in harmony.

Director: Without getting into a long discussion about it, I'd only say for now that the spirit of dialogue seeks to bring those parts into harmony. Does that make sense?

Friend: Yes. But now I have another question. You said debate is a key ingredient of freedom.

Director: Yes, I did.

Friend: But then you went on to say, in effect, that dialogue is better than debate.

Director: True.

Friend: So you believe dialogue is an even more key ingredient of freedom than debate?

Director: Of course.

Friend: Then why would anyone engage in debate when he might dialogue instead?

Director: Why are you engaging in the debate tomorrow night?

Friend: The truth? It will look good on my résumé.

Director: Well, that's one reason why someone would engage in debate when he might engage in dialogue instead.

Friend: But the debate will only last a couple of hours. I can dialogue as much as I like afterwards.

Director: But it's the preparation for debate that steals time from dialogue, Friend.

Friend: Oh, I'm not spending that much time preparing.

Director: Then you're different than most. Most people driven by the spirit of debate prepare constantly — all of their lives, in fact. I'm glad you're not one of them.

79 VIGILANCE

Director: Friend, can you read what it says on the base of that statue over there?

Friend: Sure. It says: "The price of freedom is eternal vigilance."

Director: What do you think that means?

Friend: It means we can't just assume we'll always be free.

Director: Why not?

Friend: Because there are those who would take our freedom away.

Director: So we must keep on the watch for these people?

Friend: Yes. Eternally.

Director: And where do we look for them?

Friend: What do you mean?

Director: I mean, do we watch other nations to make sure they don't try to take our freedom away?

Friend: Yes, of course we do.

Director: And don't we even appoint people whose job it is to make sure this doesn't happen?

Friend: You mean like the president and various heads of government?

Director: Yes.

Friend: Well, part of their job is no doubt to make sure we don't lose our freedom to other nations.

Director: And whose job is it to watch them, these heads of government, to make sure they're doing their jobs properly?

Friend: Who watches the watchers? We all do.

Director: What power do we have to do something if we don't like what we see?

Friend: We have the power of the vote.

Director: And don't we vote for all sorts of public officials?

Friend: Of course we do.

Director: Mustn't we watch them all to make sure they're watching out for our freedom?

Friend: Yes, it's as the statue says. Eternal vigilance.

Director: And part of that vigilance is to ensure that members of our government themselves don't try to take our freedom away?

Friend: Naturally.

Director: If one of them were trying to take our freedom from us, what's something he would be likely to do?

Friend: He would lie to us.

Director: So we, as watchers, must know when someone in government is lying?

Friend: You're right. We must know.

Director: Now how do you think we know when someone is lying?

Friend: We have to know the truth.

Director: We have a duty to learn the truth?

Friend: Of course.

Director: Do we learn, for instance, the truth about the entire tax code?

Friend: What? No, we have experts outside of government who learn that.

Director: And what about, for example, the truth about all regulated food and drugs?

Friend: Again, we have outside experts who learn that.

Director: So these outside experts watch over their areas of expertise and ensure that the government tells the truth about them?

Friend: Exactly.

Director: Who watches the outside experts?

Friend: Anyone else with expertise enough to question what they say.

Director: And since many of us have or can gain some degree of expertise in one area or another, there are always some people to keep an eye on things?

Friend: Yes.

Director: But what about the people as a whole? What must we be expert in?

Friend: The people as a whole?

Director: Yes.

Friend: I don't know that the people as a whole is expert in anything, Director. Individuals are experts.

Director: But the whole of the people is made up of individuals, isn't it? I'll tell you what I'm getting at. It's something that's been troubling me while we've been speaking. Vigilance is for the sake of freedom, right?

Friend: Right. But what's troubling about that?

Director: Nothing — provided we know what freedom is.

Friend: That's what the people must be expert in? Freedom?

Director: Yes. And don't you agree? I mean, can any amount of vigilance do any good if the people don't know what freedom is?

Friend: No, it can't. You're right. We all must be fully expert in freedom.

Director: But what if not all of us know freedom that well?

Friend: Then those who don't might open the door, even if unintentionally, to those who would take our freedom away.

Director: So is there anything more important to a free people than ensuring that as many people as possible know, truly know, what freedom is?

Friend: Nothing is more important.

Director: Then let's do what we can to help them know.